Alan Butler has spent 30 years immersed in world history, writing books delving into neglected recesses of the past, including ancient cosmology. Three of his books written with co-author Christopher Knight have attained cult status: *Civilization One* (2004), *Before the Pyramids* (2009) and *The Hiram Key Revisited* (2010), all published by Watkins. His most recent title was *Rosslyn Chapel Decoded* (with John Ritchie; published by Watkins, 2013).

# The Dawn of Genius

## *The Minoan Super-Civilization and the Truth About Atlantis*

### Alan Butler

WATKINS PUBLISHING
LONDON

This edition first published in the UK and USA 2014 by
Watkins Publishing Limited
PO Box 883
Oxford, OX1 9PL
UK

A member of Osprey Group

For enquiries in the USA and Canada:
Osprey Publishing
PO Box 3985
New York, NY 10185-3985
Tel: (001) 212 753 4402
Email: info@ospreypublishing.com

1 3 5 7 9 10 8 6 4 2

Typeset by JCS Publishing Services Ltd, www.jcs-publishing.co.uk

Printed and bound by CPI Group (UK) Ltd, Croydon, CR0 4YY

A CIP record for this book is available from the British Library

ISBN: 978-1-78028-684-6

Watkins Publishing is supporting the Woodland Trust, the UK's leading
woodland conservation charity, by funding tree-planting initiatives and
woodland maintenance.

www.watkinspublishing.co.uk

# Contents

## Chapter 1

# An Island in the Sun

At the time of writing this book it cannot be denied that the United States of America is the most powerful nation state in the world. The capital of the United States is Washington, DC, a city originally planned and commenced at the very end of the 18th century. Like any major city on the Earth, Washington, DC is something of an urban sprawl, but at its heart – in its political and economic centre – it is, without doubt, one of the most beautiful cities in the world. From the Lincoln Memorial in the west, right along the Mall to the Capitol, some of the most magnificent and even awe-inspiring architecture ever created by the hand of man is displayed for visitors and residents alike to see. All these buildings, such as the Capitol itself, the Jefferson Memorial, the White House and countless buildings given over to government, the United States' economy and institutions of learning and science, have one thing in common – they are built in a 'classical' style.

In principle this says much about fashion at the time Washington, DC was conceived. The period during which a free United States became a reality was one in which intellectuals in Europe were looking back to the great civilizations of Greece and Rome. Whilst it is true that Western taste was captured by the grace and symmetry of Greek and Roman architecture, with its soaring pillars and grand porticos, it was far from being the case that those who turned to this style of architecture were catering 'only' to a visual consideration. Rather they saw classical architecture as being representative of successful and powerful empires from the past. Even this notion was merely part of a departure in thinking that had followed the Renaissance.

The medieval period had been one of feudalism and repression. The reins of power had been held by Church and state combined. Anyone searching for truth, either spiritually or scientifically, had been liable to persecution, from repressive monarchies on the one hand and the cast-iron fist of the Roman Catholic Church on the other. With the religious Reformation that took hold from the 16th century onwards, large parts of Western Europe broke their ties with the Catholic Church. Even those areas that remained under its influence, for example Italy, became less restricted by its edicts and control. There is little doubt that many aspects of the Renaissance began specifically in the Italian city states, many of them right in the pope's back yard. An increasingly corrupt and ethically bankrupt Church looked to retrieving its possessions throughout Western Europe, and at the same time failed to see what was happening on its own doorstep.

Once the genie of enlightenment was out of its bottle, nothing that either the Church or state might do could make it return. Lacking any confidence in the institutions of its own day, intellectual thought in Western Europe began to look back, to the apparent order and visual symmetry of the ancient world. Roman architecture had survived all across the vast sway of its empire but there was little original in Roman tastes. Practically everything the Romans created in terms of both civic and religious buildings owed their style to Ancient Greece.

At the same time something quite extraordinary began to take place. Long-lost writings by Ancient Greek thinkers and statesman began to find their way into Italy and subsequently across all of Western Europe. These had probably been present all along and many of them had been preserved by Arabic scholars, who were always much less fettered when it came to learning. These documents, from philosophers, politicians and mathematicians, reflected the very best of Ancient Greek thought. They spoke of personal aspiration, of a search for truth that was unrestricted by religious thought and of political institutions that were as far from those of the repressive Western European states as chalk is from cheese.

Greek art demonstrated a search for beauty for its own sake – of the elevation of the very human form to a god-like status, whilst those of its buildings that survived showed an understanding of aesthetics allied to mathematics and geometry.

Probably most important of all, Renaissance thinking flirted with a concept practised in Ancient Greece but almost totally unknown in Europe throughout the medieval period – democracy. The notion that ordinary people could take part in the order and running of the states in which they lived must have seemed at the same time outrageous and yet deeply compelling. However, democracy did make sense to people living in some of the city states of Italy at the time. Florence, for example, practised its own form of limited democracy. Its thinkers and even its leaders would have felt they had much in common with those who fitted the fluted pillars of the Parthenon together in ancient Athens.

The thinkers of the Renaissance and after could eventually enjoy the very best and most elevated thoughts of a long-dead culture, whilst at the same time knowing virtually nothing of its true history. Although Western Europe came to idolize Ancient Greece, with its democracy, its free-thinking philosophers and its schools of scientific learning, the truth of Ancient Greece, with its habitually warring states, its total reliance on a vast reservoir of slaves and its peculiar and often cruel traditions and laws remained unknown.

Ancient Greece as it was envisioned even by the 18th century, when Washington, DC was planned, was nothing short of a myth – though like all myths it contained an element of truth. Its highest aspirations were idolized, whilst its many faults and failings were either not known or were deliberately ignored. The founding fathers of the United States, men such as George Washington and especially Thomas Jefferson, were intelligent men, committed absolutely to the enlightenment and to the very highest aspirations of Ancient Greece as they saw them. They deliberately copied elements of both Greek and Roman republicanism for their own free state – once Britain had been beaten and the colonies could stand alone. As an example, the very structure where democracy operated and where the new state's laws were laid down was called 'The Capitol', a reference to the Capitoline Hill in Rome, which was always seen as being the sacred and administrative heart of the Roman Empire. One of the legislative bodies of the United States' republican democracy was and is named the Senate, another word derived directly from the Roman model of government, which itself owed much to Ancient

Greece. In other words, the new United States republic based itself almost wholly and with pride on a quite seriously misunderstood version of an ancient world that was actually far from the paradise perceived.

Roman government, even during the republic, was despotic, cruel and on many occasions downright barbaric. Later, during the empire, Rome was ruled by a number of powerful factions and families, from which the emperors were drawn. With its reliance on slavery, its deplorable treatment of women, its flagrant disregard of the rights of its own people – not to mention those of the regions it conquered – Ancient Rome probably represents just about the worst role model for modern government imaginable. Ancient Greece, which consisted of hundreds of warring states, was hardly any better. In truth, both in the Greek city states and in Rome, only a tiny handful of citizens ever had any right to participate in government and the majority of individuals were studiously ignored and mistreated.

To the founders of the free United States, and to shakers and movers in other parts of America and back in Western Europe, none of this mattered – in the main probably because they were not aware of the true history of either Greece or Rome. Like all generations, they viewed the history that suited them, and even if their notions of history were at odds with reality, their aspirations on behalf of humanity were quite genuine.

Nevertheless, there was one area of both Greek and Roman ancient history that did play a very important part in the recovery of Western Europe from the repression it had experienced ever since the end of the old Roman Empire. This lay in the study of science – and the acquisition of genuine knowledge for its own sake.

The gradual proliferation of Ancient Greek and Roman books, most of which had been preserved in Arabic translations, now appearing in other European languages introduced much of Western Europe to concepts that had lain dormant for many centuries. A good example of this was astronomy. Catholic dogma always insisted that the Earth was the centre of the solar system, whereas the Ancient Greeks had known very well that this was not the case. As the power of the Church declined, there were scholars trained in Greek and Roman learning who could rapidly recreate the solar system in its true form. This led to a gradual understanding of planetary size and movement – and a view of the solar system and of the cosmos that owed nothing to religious doctrine.

Grand architecture, which for centuries had been the prerogative of the Church and powerful rulers, now gave up its secrets, and along with them geometry and mathematics became better understood outside of cloisters and castles. Experimentation became the norm. Previously anyone mixing chemical compounds stood a good chance of being accused of sorcery. Greek and Roman medical treatises became available, offering new incentives and information to those who sought to alleviate the ills of humanity, whilst political and philosophical thought underwent a transformation previously unknown in Europe.

There can be little doubt that all of this came as a legacy from Ancient Greece and Rome, but since almost everything Rome knew or cherished was originally Greek we clearly need to look towards the Eastern Mediterranean and the Aegean for the foundation of our modern world. Despite the misunderstandings of the 18th-century mind regarding many elements of the Greco-Roman past, one only has to look at the architecture of Western European and American towns and cities to understand just how very significant these cultures have been.

If there is a problem here, it stems from the use of the word 'Ancient' to describe the city states of Greece, which genuinely did exist several centuries before the modern era. Whilst in a linguistic sense it is appropriate to refer to the culture as ancient, advances in our understanding of history now clearly demonstrate that Ancient Greece did not spring, full blooded and complete, from nothing. The Ancient Greece and Rome which we still hold in a sort of reverence were both Iron Age cultures, whereas European history goes back beyond this, through the extremely important Bronze Age to the Stone Age. In comparison with the span of humanity, Ancient Greece is actually very recent. Everything it embodied sprang from 'something else'; what is more, Ancient Greece itself was only gradually reconstructed after a 'dark age' that had lasted for centuries.

This book represents an attempt to show from where the Greeks, and ultimately the Romans, derived their knowledge, their religion and even their concept of democracy. The Greeks knew very well, and often admitted, that they had not been the first culture of note in the Eastern Mediterranean, though an absolute knowledge of where their own 'parent' culture had actually been situated seems to have been lost to them. This is not surprising because by the time the Greeks looked around to find it, the evidence lay under countless mounds of earth and broken pottery shards, not to mention beneath the waves of the Mediterranean itself.

Now the truth of the situation is making itself known, and in order to understand where Greek knowledge and civilization developed, which in turn has given so much to our modern world, we have to look to the south of modern Greece, to a large island which is today known as Crete.

## Crete: Jewel of the Eastern Mediterranean

The vast majority of people arriving in Crete these days are holidaymakers. They make landfall at one of the island's airports and if they arrive during daylight hours, visitors gaze in rapture at the azure blue sea, the white mountains and the fertile plains and valleys as their aircraft makes its final approach to Herakllion, Chania or Sitia.

Crete is the second largest island in the Eastern Mediterranean and is situated to the south of mainland Greece, where the Aegean gives way to the Libyan Sea. The islands of the Mediterranean are by no means similar to each other. Some are relatively flat, others are more mountainous but fairly sparse in terms of vegetation and many are quite arid, especially in the summer months. Partly because of its size and also on account of the nature of its climate, Crete is one of the most verdant of the Mediterranean islands. It is extremely mountainous, which means that it also offers plateaus, valleys and gorges, all of which are rich in vegetation.

Many parts of Crete have deep-red soils and the island is incredibly fertile. I was proudly told by a local on my first visit there, now well over 30 years ago, that almost any seed or seedling placed into Crete's rich, volcanic earth can be guaranteed to grow. Every conceivable crop and fruit seems to flourish somewhere on the island and, thanks to greenhouses, even bananas are cultivated in abundance. To taste a Cretan tomato or courgette, with its unique flavour born of the verdant soil, the almost incessant sunlight and fresh, mountain-filtered water, is an experience in itself, whilst the sea around Crete is exploited for marine food of every conceivable sort. To any holidaymaker who thinks beyond the burger bars and fried chicken outlets, Crete represents a culinary heaven, made all the more appealing by its locally grown olives and succulent lamb, provided by sheep that live a peaceful life, grazing on the diverse herbage of the hill slopes.

Like any holiday resort Crete offers a wealth of possibilities. Some visitors never wish to wander far from the excellent beaches, strung out along a north coast that extends, with its many harbours and indentations, for the island's whole 260-kilometre length. Again, like its Mediterranean and Greek island counterparts, Crete is the centre of a thriving youth holiday culture. Its many towns and resorts sport clubs and bars that, during the season, are open throughout the night. So for many the holiday progresses from beach to bar, from bar to club and then home in the early hours before hitting the beach again by lunch time. I have personally talked to summer visitors who have never strayed a single kilometre from their hotel and beach during the full two-week holiday.

However, to really appreciate what Crete is about, it is probably necessary to keep slightly more regular hours – to rise early in the morning and to set off, on foot, by car or on highly entertaining public transport, in order to explore one of the many hundreds of historical sites, natural wonders, quaint mountain villages, intriguing caverns, steep-sided gorges or olive-covered mountain slopes of this incredible place.

It is on such journeys that the true size and scale of Crete is appreciated and it is also the mobile visitor who gains the most from meeting with and talking to the Cretans themselves. Crete is, of course, now a part of Greece, though throughout its often stormy past it has been controlled by a number of different cultures. And though the Cretans are proud of their present Greek heritage, there is also something quite different about them: an independence and a sense of freedom that sets them apart, no matter what language they happen to speak these days.

By the standards of those of us who come from much more western and northern parts of Europe, Crete is blessed with a wonderful climate. It can become extremely hot in the summer months, though near the sea and in the mountains it is comfortable rather than oppressive. Travel to Crete in the winter and you will find cooler days and somewhat chilly nights. In December or January the locals walk around in thick woollen pullovers and shiver in temperatures that would represent an extremely pleasant spring or autumn day in my native Britain. To ward off the cold in winter the more elderly men frequent village tavernas by the middle of the morning and sit on ancient chairs by the roadside, sipping or gulping from small glasses of raki, a highly potent spirit flavoured with aniseed and herbs. The very aroma of raki anywhere in the world takes me immediately back to those quaint little white villages, nestling in the folds of mountains or at the head of narrow, green valleys, where the only sound during the still, hot days is the chirrup of cicadas and the soft, distant jangle of sheep bells.

To the mainland Greeks of long ago, Crete was reckoned to be the birthplace of their most powerful deity, Zeus, who could hurl thunderbolts at unsuspecting mortals or even his fellow deities. It's no wonder he was thought to have come from Crete. On any dark, summer night, the clouds can creep in, unseen. Suddenly, there is a slight thrill in the air that is almost indescribable, and often this is the only advance warning of a sudden simultaneous flash and a crash of epic proportions that bounces between the mountains, so loud it sounds as though the very island is rending itself in two.

Moments later the rain comes down in monsoon-like torrents. Buildings quake as the wrath of Zeus breaks time and again across the landscape, with huge lightning flashes allowing momentary, ghostly and acutely monochromatic views of distant vistas. Despite the apparent terror of some visitors, the locals smile. They welcome the violent summer storms with their ferocious rain. Crete has streams, though nothing that could be referred to as rivers. Rain water drips down into natural aquifers and provides the necessary drinking water for people, animals and plants. There is also significant rainfall at times in winter – all part of the natural cycle that has, for thousands of years, made Crete into the paradise it is.

When I first visited the island, Crete was a much quieter place generally than a visitor will find it in high season these days. What was the small village of Malia, where I first stayed and enjoyed the delights of Crete, is now a thriving tourist town. But it's still only a five-minute drive up the mountain and then less than an hour to the Plain of Lisithi, high in the mountains. How many times I have stood at its rim, staring out across the little fields at so many locally built windmills that the place looks like something out of Cervantes' *Don Quixote*. In the distance is Mount Dicte, part of a long range of mountains and hills that protect the plain and which rise high above the coastal regions.

It was in Mount Dicte that the Greeks believed their father god, Zeus, had been born, the son of the great god Cronos and his wife Rhea. Other legends point to a cave in Mount Idi, some kilometres distant, but all the tales agree that Zeus was placed on Crete for safety from his tyrannical and jealous father. There he was nurtured by a she-goat, until he grew to manhood and overthrew his father to become king of the gods. It is possible to visit the caves associated with Zeus, and the area is popular in summer because it is sometimes pleasant to get away from what can be stifling heat.

The south of Crete is also worth visiting, though it has a generally rocky coast and does not attract tourists to the same extent as the north coast. Here there are other mythological tales, of Sirens and Cyclops. Sirens were believed to lure sailors to their doom by pretending to be beautiful maidens, whilst the Cyclops were ferocious one-eyed giants who would capture unsuspecting travellers and ate human flesh.

Back in the 1980s, if one took a drive into the more remote regions on a Sunday, it was possible to see old men sunning themselves in the village streets, sometimes adorned with belts of bullets, kept safe for decades after the Second World War. Crete was occupied by the forces of the Axis and, together with British forces left behind after Crete was overrun, the locals fought a ferocious guerrilla campaign, despite the fact that local civilians suffered terribly as a result. This typifies the Cretan nature, to whom freedom is everything. How many times when these elderly men were still alive I heard the expression which all Cretan males were willing to express: 'Better dead than a slave'.

The reason Axis forces were so keen to gain and retain control of Crete was because of its strategic position. Located in the eastern part of the Mediterranean, it makes an ideal base from which to influence Greece and the southern Balkans to the north. Forces located in Crete can also regulate traffic to the east and the coast of the Levant, as well as controlling access to the Western Mediterranean. Crete became of even greater importance once the Suez Canal was opened in 1869. The Suez Canal is a shortcut that allows vessels to pass from Western Europe, via the Mediterranean Sea, into the Red Sea and the Arabian Sea beyond it, without having to travel all the way around the southern coast of Africa. Crete is strategically placed to the north-west of the Suez Canal and in the narrowest part of the Mediterranean, allowing naval forces stationed in its outstanding natural harbours to influence and even control international commerce.

Although the Suez Canal is less than two centuries old, the excellent geographical location of Crete was not lost on whoever wished to influence trade in the region, extending back not hundreds but thousands of years. This is one of the reasons why Crete has been so influenced by other European cultures. After its fascinating Minoan period, which we will deal with presently, it was settled by the Mycenaean Greeks. The Greeks were followed by the Romans – who held an empire that made control of the Mediterranean absolutely crucial.

At the end of the Roman era Crete fell under the influence of Arab rulers, before eventually being captured by the Venetians in the early 13th century. The Venetians remained in control for almost four centuries and the island became very prosperous, before the massive Ottoman Empire gained control of Crete in 1669. By 1821 Greece as a whole was fighting for its independence and the island of Crete was no exception. Decades of bitter struggle followed but Crete eventually gained its own government in 1898. In 1913 Crete opted to become part of the greater Greek state and has been administered as such ever since, except for the period between 1941 and the end of the Second World War, when Crete was controlled by Germany.

Crete is the home of many archaeological and historic sites, from periods extending back well over four thousand years. The best known of these is the ruins of the Palace of Knossos, first excavated by the British Arthur Evans in the early years of the 20th century. It was the unearthing of Knossos that led to the rediscovery of the Minoans, though in reality this is not the name members of the civilization gave themselves. Evans named the Minoans after the mythical King Minos, who is mentioned in Greek legends. The Minoans were indisputably Europe's first 'super civilization'. By as early as 2000 BC the island was trading far and wide across the Mediterranean and up into the Aegean. The Minoan civilization had good relations with most of the surrounding cultures, and even sent ambassadors to Ancient Egypt.

Minoan Crete had outposts in mainland Greece, Italy, almost certainly in southern Spain and also at the far eastern end of the Mediterranean, along the coast of the Levant.

## The British Isles

The southern shores of the British Isles are over 2,700 kilometres north-west of Crete, but that is the distance that would be traversed by a modern passenger plane. By sea the distance from Crete to the British Isles is nearer five thousand kilometres. Whilst the British Isles are far bigger than Crete, they are also 20° further north; Crete is washed by the azure Mediterranean, but the British Isles suffer the ravages of Atlantic seas to the west and on the eastern side are battered by the North Sea, which is recognized as being one of the most treacherous and stormy stretches of water in the world.

Like Crete, the British Isles are verdant and green. True, the climate is nowhere near as mild as it is in the Mediterranean and the winters can be particularly harsh, especially towards the north, but even the very earliest farmers had no difficulty growing a range of crops or raising a multitude of animals. Early human habitation in the British Isles was a spasmodic affair. During the time humans have been present on the Earth, the climate in the British Isles has fluctuated dramatically, leading to some periods during ice ages when our early hunter-gatherer ancestors must have retreated back to more southerly latitudes.

However, by the time the Minoan civilization was growing and flourishing in far-off Crete, the British Isles were also doing well – though in a very different way. This period, towards the end of the Stone Age and into the Bronze Age, is a difficult one when it comes to knowing exactly what was taking place in the British Isles. A wet climate and acidic soils have not always been kind to archaeologists, whose only real glimpse of such a remote period on the very fringes of Western Europe comes from what these ancient people lost, abandoned or deliberately buried.

It might be assumed that life in Britain as a whole around 2000 BC was probably not so different than it appeared to be by the time the Romans invaded the larger of the British Isles early in the modern era. They found a place dotted with generally small villages and split into tribal homelands.

The British Isles at the beginning of the Roman period was a place of agriculture (which is one of the reasons why the Romans wished to control the place). The people living across the islands were called 'Celts' by the Romans. They were an independent, aggressive and quarrelsome bunch – as likely to wage war against each other as to unite to fight the Roman invaders. By the time of the Roman invasion of AD 43 some of the bigger, more southerly British tribes were beginning to use coinage and regularly traded, both with other tribes and with outsiders, but across the British Isles as a whole there was no sense of unity and the British Celts never created what today would be considered a 'civilization'.

Paradoxically, the very presence of the Roman invaders did cause at least some tribes to work together for a common goal but the historic enmity between many of them made it possible for the Romans to establish control over what is today England, Scotland and Wales – as much by political expediency and clever manipulation as by force of arms.

Two thousand years before the Romans arrived, the landscape of the British Isles would probably have been outwardly very similar. The main difference lay in the population. The people the Romans knew as the Celts did not begin to arrive in Britain until the Iron Age. It is generally accepted that they began to settle around 600 BC. Prior to this the British Isles were occupied by people about whom we know far less. The Stone Age and Bronze Age Britons spoke a different language, undoubtedly had different beliefs and practices and certainly behaved in a very different way compared to the later Celts.

The Celtic British Isles were a place of tribal interest and conflict, whereas going back to before 1500–2000 BC there is strong evidence of a much more integrated and co-operative population – one that was almost certainly less warlike. From the northernmost islands of Scotland, down to the tip of southern England and from the far west, right across to the North Sea, the British Isles are still covered by the evidence that our Stone Age and Bronze Age ancestors had a commonality of purpose that the Celts never knew. Beginning as early as 3500 BC, the people of the region began to create massive structures across the landscape. At first these were usually straight ceremonial tracks, sometimes extending for many kilometres. Soon these were complemented by circular earthworks, known as 'henges'.

Henges are distinguished by having banks and ditches, with one or more entrances. There must originally have been many hundreds if not thousands of henges and some of them were colossal in size. In the north of England, near the city of Ripon, there is still to be seen an array of three giant henges. They stretch in a line across relatively flat landscape, from north-west to south-east and each of the Thornborough henges is so large it would be easily possible to fit a cathedral as large as St Paul's into it. This undertaking alone was of epic proportions – around 3500 BC, it is impossible to imagine that it could have been achieved by a small, local population. Estimates vary, but it is unlikely that at this time there were more than a hundred thousand people living in the whole of the British Isles. All of these people had to be fed; this was achieved by subsistence farming, which would have taken up a great deal of everyone's time. Resourcing the many thousands of hours necessary to create something on the scale of the Thornborough henges would surely have meant bringing in individuals from significant distances to help.

Nor were these the only giant henges, even in this part of the British landscape. There were others in the vicinity, just as large and just as time consuming to create. In some areas of the British Isles passage graves of a similar age to the henges are also to be found. These too are monumental structures, built in stone and covered over with great mounds of earth. Within a few centuries in Britain people had begun to drag huge stones around the landscape. These were carefully erected in circles (sometimes overlying earlier henges) or in avenues or other alignments. Most of these stones were pounded into regularity using stone mauls; on occasions they were dragged across moor and mountain for many kilometres to adorn what must have been deeply sacred sites. It is anyone's guess how many stone circles once stood on the British Isles but since hundreds still remain, it must have been a significant number.

The people of the British Isles were not alone in these endeavours. The western shores of France, and in particular Brittany, carry similar monuments, together with amazing rows of stones that stretch for kilometres, and which date to more or less the same period as the stone circles. What all this effort was for is a question in its own right, but what must immediately be obvious is that these astounding feats could never have been contemplated without a tremendous level of co-operation on the part of the indigenous population. Even more astounding is the evidence that exactly the same units of linear measurement were used to construct these monuments, from the north of Scotland to the south of England and in Brittany, over a period of two thousand years.

There is little evidence of widespread warfare or violence across the British Isles during the long period that the henges and stone circles were being created. Burials of powerful warrior chiefs are absent until a much later date, and large defensive structures, such as the later Iron Age hill forts, are not in evidence. It is clear that most of the communal effort of the people at the end of the Stone Age and during the early Bronze Age was devoted to sizeable, communal projects that must certainly have had both a civic and a religious significance. In reality they were probably too busy co-operating in the creation of these masterpieces to contemplate petty, tribal disputes.

By the time Minoan Crete was establishing some of its most distant outposts in the Mediterranean and creating its huge palaces at home, great structures such as Avebury and Stonehenge were nearing their completion in southern Britain. One might reasonably suggest that two such apparently different cultures, though existing at the same period, could surely have had very few parallels This is exactly what I would have thought, had I not been provided with evidence that, as far apart as the British Isles and Crete were, significant links did exist between the two cultures. It is these connections I want to examine in this book, in order to establish a new understanding of European prehistory and its ultimate legacy.

A more recent connection between the British Isles and Minoan Crete also turns out to be highly significant. It comes in the form of a Victorian gentleman by the name of Arthur Evans.

## Chapter 2

# The Hill of Knossos

The science of archaeology as it is known and understood today is effectively a 20th-century invention. This is not to suggest that people in earlier periods failed to take an interest in the past. On the contrary, as the age of enlightenment dawned in the 18th century, a fascination with ancient history, and particularly of classical Greece and Rome, reached fever pitch in Western Europe. In particular the chance rediscovery, in 1748, of the ruins of Pompeii in Italy – a Roman city buried in a volcanic eruption in AD 79 – spawned an interest in the classical past that had much to do with the almost fanatical obsession with classicism that followed in art and architecture. However, those who first excavated sites such as Pompeii were, essentially, treasure seekers. Objects were rived from the ground with little or no understanding of context (the way one object relates to other associated finds) and apart from a known event, such as that at Pompeii, little or no attention was paid to the accurate dating of historical finds anywhere.

Of particular importance to antiquarians of the 18th and much of the 19th century were 'collections'. These were invariably held in private hands, usually those of the rich and influential. A particular individual might go to great trouble to put together a collection of Greek vases, or Roman statuary, which would often be displayed for the benefit of the collector and perhaps his friends. In their anxiety to add to such collections, their owners were not usually too particular about how new acquisitions were obtained – or from where. As a result, a wealth of invaluable information regarding all manner of cultures was lost forever, as treasure hunters digging on any given site ignored everything they encountered which they considered to be of no material value.

In reality we probably have to be slightly charitable to those concerned. It took a very long time and a great deal of accumulated experience to catalogue the rediscovered past in a way that allowed even a rough dating of truly ancient objects to take place. Even then it was often difficult, if not impossible, to achieve anything more than an educated guess. Real accuracy in dating only became possible with extremely modern techniques, such as carbon dating. As a result, in the case of the classical cultures, a great deal of reliance was placed upon known, written historical sources, which often owed as much to legend as they did to fact. As an example, the story of the siege and the sacking of Troy, as described from Ancient Greek sources, was taken, by some at least, as being an expression of a genuine, historical event. As a result, the finds of the German Heinrich Schliemann (1822–90) at Hisserlik, Turkey in the 1870s were immediately attributed to the story of Troy, though with little or no factual evidence to back such a claim.

If it was difficult to understand historical finds from known cultures, which had left literary sources, how much more difficult was it to unravel the puzzles created by the sort of historical discoveries that were made in a place such as Britain?

A local landowner might busy himself robbing a whole series of burial mounds on his estate and would happily lump together everything he found into the ubiquitous 'collection', without the slightest idea as to the reality of an extremely long British prehistory. The burial mounds he pillaged could have represented a broad cross-section of ancient history, from the early Bronze Age to the late Iron Age, on the way taking in several related or unrelated cultures, but to the collector they were all merely part of a shadowy prehistory about which little or nothing was known.

In the main, to the 18th-century antiquarian, it was gold, silver, statuary and the like that was of the greatest interest, whilst the simple, fragile elements of everyday life that had managed to survive were generally cast aside as worthless. Times have definitely changed and it would be fair to say that to a modern archaeologist, the contents of an ancient village midden (a dump of domestic waste) might be far more precious that a random piece of jewellery or even a hoard of coins.

One of the greatest of the well-heeled treasure-hunters, by this time in the 19th century, was a man I have already mentioned briefly. His name was Heinrich Schliemann, and though nobody these days would consider him to be truly worthy of the title 'archaeologist', he did do a great deal to popularize the idea of a concerted and organized 'dig' to unravel secrets from the past.

Schliemann was born in 1822, in what is now Germany, the son of a Protestant minister. Although the family was not rich, Heinrich's father was well educated; Ernst Schliemann took a great interest in his children and so young Heinrich learned a great many of his earliest lessons at his father's knee. It was during these formative years that Heinrich was regaled with

Ancient Greek stories, particularly those from the *Odyssey* and the *Iliad*. These were tales he never forgot.

As well as being fascinated with history, it turned out that Heinrich Schliemann had a good head for business. After a spell as a cabin boy in merchant ships, at 22 years of age he began to work for an import and export business in Hamburg. He quickly showed his acumen and the company sent him as its representative to St Petersburg in Russia. Eventually, he followed his brother, Ludwig, to the recently discovered gold fields of California in the United States. There, instead of prospecting himself, Heinrich saw the banking opportunities that all the new wealth offered. He formed his own bank and quickly became extremely rich.

Eventually tiring of the United States, despite having gained citizenship, Schliemann returned to Russia, married, and went on to make several more fortunes. He had an excellent eye for any opportunity that came his way and by 1858, though only 36 years of age, he decided to retire from business and to devote himself to a passion that had not diminished since his childhood – Heinrich Schliemann decided to devote the remainder of his life and his great fortune to finding the fabled city of Troy.

The epic tale of the siege and eventual sacking of the fabulous city of Troy by the Greeks is the subject matter of the *Iliad*, attributed to the Ancient Greek writer Homer, who lived around the 8th century BC. At the time of Heinrich Schliemann many scholars had come to consider the story of Troy to be entirely fictitious, so the concept of setting out to find such a place seemed ludicrous, but this did nothing to deter Schliemann. He had his money and his dream – and more than a few leads at his disposal.

Working on the advice of an expatriate English amateur archaeologist, Frank Calvert, Schliemann eventually settled on a location in Turkey, known as Hissarlik – a mound that had already revealed archaeological finds. There, together with his second wife, the 17-year-old Sophie Engastromenus, Schliemann began digging in 1871. Without any formal training – in fairness, archaeology was in its infancy – Heinrich Schliemann adopted the methods of the 18th-century treasure hunter. He dug a huge trench, working quickly through the levels where the Homeric Troy had actually been and on down to a period a thousand years earlier. There he discovered a fortune in sumptuous gold jewellery and adornments, which he incorrectly called 'Priam's treasure' in deference to the story told in the *Iliad*.

Although he didn't realize it at the time, Schliemann had discovered not one but several Troys, the oldest dating back to the Bronze Age. His methods were crude and he has since been accused of destroying Troy more successfully and completely than the Greeks ever did. Nevertheless, the treasures made him a household name. In addition to carrying out several further excavations at Hissarlik he also became fascinated by the Mycenaean civilization on the Greek mainland and conducted digs there that revealed shaft graves and further treasures. By the late 1880s he had contracted a severe inner-ear infection, which eventually took his life on 26 December 1890.

A young man growing up in far-off England had followed the exploits of Heinrich Schliemann closely, though in terms of nature and methodology the two men were entirely different. Arthur Evans was born in 1851 in Hampshire and was Heinrich Schliemann's junior by nearly 30 years. His father was a partner in a family-owned paper mill, which made John Evans reasonably prosperous by the standards of the time.

The family fortune made it possible for John Evans to indulge his children. As a result Arthur attended a very good local preparatory school, before being sent to Harrow, one of Britain's foremost public schools. Even by the time he arrived there, young Arthur already had a great love for history. His father was a keen collector of ancient artifacts, amassing a peerless collection which was eventually given to the Ashmolean Museum in Oxford. As a child, and later into adulthood, Arthur had roamed the countryside with his father, seeking out new specimens for the collection and trying to understand the fearfully difficult twists and turns of Ancient British history.

After receiving a degree in history from Brasenose College, Oxford, Arthur, who, though short in stature, was of a robust constitution, set out on a series of journeys that would eventually lead him to Crete. Together with a friend, and subsequently with his brother, Arthur Evans spent months walking through the troubled Balkans. He eventually became a reporter for the *Manchester Guardian* and his articles on the precarious political situation – as the Ottoman Empire began to dissolve and new factions, both political and religious, sought to gain control of the region – proved popular. His journalistic sympathies were always with the underdog, though it has been suggested that in reality he acted as an official, or more likely an unofficial, spy for the British government. On more than one occasion he was arrested and even imprisoned, but there always seemed to be some influential person to call on and he completed this phase of his fascinating life unscathed.

After a period back in Britain, with his new wife Margaret, Evans was eventually made the keeper of the Ashmolean Museum, which had been based around the collections of

Elias Ashmole (1617–92), an antiquarian and politician. The institution was being overhauled and revamped. Thanks to Evans it would henceforth concentrate on archaeological exhibits. A sedentary life didn't suit Arthur at all, and his new position allowed great scope for travel, in order to obtain new exhibits for the museum. So, after some excavations in Kent, to prove his worth as an archaeologist, he set off again, travelling to Athens. He rejoined his wife in Bordighera, where she had been staying with her sister, but on the way home she had a reoccurrence of an earlier illness and died in Italy. Arthur was devastated. He never remarried, even though he was only in his forties at this time. Instead he devoted the remainder of his life to ancient history and archaeology.

In 1894, a year after Margaret's death, Arthur Evans heard again of a location he had been told about some years previously. It was a hill, near the north shore of the island of Crete, which had already yielded some potentially interesting finds. Evans had come across an interesting and previously unknown script on seal stones he had purchased in mainland Greece. At the time he had been told these had originated in Crete, and the thought of possibly uncovering a previously unknown Greek culture fascinated him.

Crete was in turmoil, with one political or religious group playing itself off against another. Obtaining the necessary land for the excavations was proving to be tortuously difficult, thanks to the political intrigues caused by so many differing interests. Evans, with the political skill and diplomacy he had already amassed, found a way through the red tape. Using money that had come to him on the death of a relative he was able to secure part of the hill, ready to begin excavating. Somewhat earlier Heinrich Schliemann, whom Evans had met, had tried to secure the Cretan site but without any success. Evans was more circumspect than the somewhat-impatient Schliemann and, after arduous and lengthy negotiations, managed to secure himself the work that would absorb him for the remainder of his long life.

The hill in question was named after a local settlement, Kephala, but in reality it wasn't a hill at all. Rather it represented the accumulated debris of a once-huge and glorious series of buildings. When the excavation began, in 1900, Evans had no idea as to its true extent. What he did know was that Roman coins had been found all over the site at various times, some of which bore a representation of the Minotaur.

The Minotaur was a half-man, half-bull hybrid, long known about from Greek mythology and particularly from the Roman poet Ovid (43 BC–AD17/18). Ovid related that in far-off times Crete had been ruled by a great king, whose name was Minos. Minos had to fight his own brothers to retain his throne and Ovid said that the king had prayed to the god Poseidon to send him a white bull, as proof of the God's acceptance of his right to rule. The bull eventually arrived, with instructions that it was to be sacrificed to Poseidon. King Minos considered the bull to be the most wonderful creature he had ever seen and soon became determined to keep it. At the expected sacrifice he substituted another animal, and thus attracted the wrath of the great Poseidon. In revenge, and on behalf of Poseidon, the goddess Aphrodite (goddess of love) caused Pasiphaë, the wife of Minos, to fall in love with the white bull. Their love was consummated and the result was a half-human, half-bull son that became known as the Minotaur.

Although Pasiphaë wished to keep her unnatural child, this proved to be quite impossible. As it grew, the Minotaur became huge and ferocious. Being neither truly bovine nor human the Minotaur soon took to eating meat, eventually preferring the flesh of human beings. In desperation King Minos asked the Oracle at Delphi what he should do with such a monster and was told to build a huge labyrinth next to his Palace of Knossos. There the Minotaur would roam the many rooms and corridors, capturing and eating the virgin men and women that Minos demanded from the Greek mainland as tribute. The story suggested that Minos had a powerful navy and that he exercised a great deal of control in the Aegean and the Mediterranean. According to Ovid's tale, the Minotaur was eventually killed by the Greek hero Theseus.

Arthur Evans was not the first individual to reason that, as close as it was to the modern capital of Crete, Heraklion, and in such a good geographical position relative to the prosperous north coast of the island, the ruins on Kephala hill might well represent those of the ancient Cretan palace known to history as Knossos. The Roman coins seemed to point to this conclusion, because in addition to the portrait of the Minotaur on one side, they carried the word 'Knosion' on the reverse.

Obviously the story of Minos, the Minotaur and the hero Theseus could not be true, but doubtless Evans cast his mind back to the experiences of Heinrich Schliemann. Practically everyone had laughed when Schliemann suggested that the story of the sacking of Troy was more than a simple myth – until he actually went on to find the fabled city (which incidentally had been destroyed on more than one occasion.) With this in mind, the same experts who had initially ridiculed Schliemann were far less likely to dismiss evidence from mythological sources by 1900.

Some of the first finds made by Evans were artistically rendered bull's horns that had once adorned whatever buildings had stood on the site. These acted as further evidence that there might be at least a grain of truth somewhere in the story of the Minotaur. When he eventually went on to discover frescoes containing great bulls, as well as decorative bull's head ritual vessels, there seemed to be little doubt that a connection did exist between this site and the fabled stories of Knossos and the labyrinth.

Another connection that links the ruins at Kephala with the labyrinth and therefore the legend of Minos is the presence of double-headed axes associated with the building's adornment. These were used on roof lines and are also to be found etched into stones from the site. There is an interesting linguistic connection associated with the double-headed axes. The word 'labyrinth', which is taken these days to describe a maze, comes from the Lydian word 'labrys' which actually means double-headed axe. In other words, although labyrinth is now synonymous with a maze, this is not its original meaning and the presence of so many double-headed axes associated with the site in Crete might seem to be a sort of visual pun. What it actually means is that what we now call the Palace of Knossos would have been referred to by the Ancient Minoans as 'the hall of the double-headed axes'.

The double-headed axe is a symbol from prehistory that seems to have been revered right across Europe, as far as Britain in the far west. Extremely beautiful polished double-headed axes date right back to the Stone Age and for centuries they seem to have been directly associated with burials. The British examples tend to be of stone and were clearly never used, either for war or for domestic chores, but were ritual objects.

The double-headed axe probably had overtones of high status, such as kingship, but also clearly retained a symbolic and/or religious significance and it would appear that this was also the case at least as far east as the Greek world. Since Cretan art so frequently associates the double-headed axe with a female character and because double-headed axes also adorn shrines to a female deity right across Crete, it has been assumed by many experts that, on the island at least, the double-headed axe was a symbol of what seems to have been an all-powerful Cretan goddess.

When work commenced in 1900 nobody could have had the slightest idea of just how large and impressive the Palace of Knossos would turn out to be. Week by week, month by month, as more and more rooms were excavated, with their interlinking corridors, it became obvious why the building had attracted the reputation of being a maze. It is amazing to realize how long it is possible for race memories to survive. The buildings on the hill of Kephala fell into ruins, perhaps as early as 1200 BC and yet over a thousand years later, the Romans who came to rule the place clearly had at least some idea of what the palace had once been like.

Although the ruins excavated by Evans are referred to as a palace, the term is quite misleading. No royal family, no matter how grand it may have been, could ever have required living quarters on the scale of what was found at Knossos. Rather, the site had developed from being a Neolithic town into a series of buildings, only a small proportion of which would have been needed to house a ruling elite or a powerful priesthood. On the main site alone Evans eventually found 1,300 rooms, the remaining contents of which showed conclusively that most had never been living quarters at all.

Rather most of the space had been taken up by workshops, administrative centres or storerooms.

The rooms of the building had surrounded a large central court, which was paved and obviously had had a ceremonial purpose. Some parts of the so-called palace had risen to a staggering five floors around the court and light had been ingeniously supplied to inner rooms below thanks to deliberately created 'light wells' and by the use of removable walls that could section off specific parts of the larger rooms.

Some areas, such as the one Evans christened the 'throne room' were doubtless used for religious and perhaps important civic purposes. There is strong evidence that 'someone' presided in these apartments, rather than simply living in them. As its name suggests, the throne room contained a sumptuously made throne, surmounted by strange, mythical creatures, and the whole had been wonderfully decorated in bright colours and geometric patterns. Evans rebuilt parts of the palace as he envisaged it must once have looked. For this he has been both praised and deeply criticized. And whilst it is true that parts of the re-creation may have more to do with the prevalent tastes in architecture that predominated in Evan's own period, there remains little doubt that he went to every possible trouble to create a faithful representation. At worst the re-creations offer a glimpse of the lost world of the Minoans and offer a reference point to visitors, instead of a confusing and vast array of fallen walls which appear to have no sense or context.

Beyond the ostentation of the 'State Rooms' the complex at Knossos was a functional structure, which replaced the earlier Neolithic settlement. Amidst the many rooms, and especially in what appear to have been the lower or basement areas,

Evans found evidence of goods being stored in great amounts. Large jars or 'pithoi' had once contained honey, olive oil, wine and other food stuffs. There was evidence of gold and silver working, of pottery making and bronze smelting. All of this had taken place on such a huge scale that Evans was forced to conclude that it could not all have been intended to support the inhabitants of the palace, no matter how many people may have been living there.

From the outset the buildings had been supplied with a superb drainage system, which included flushing toilets in some places; the size of the drainage ditches leading away from the site indicated the possibility of there once having been as many as ten thousand people inhabiting the site. It is inconceivable that so many people could ever have been dedicated to running a royal palace and, in any case, as we shall come to discuss, there isn't the smallest shred of evidence that Minoan Crete ever had a royal family that needed housing in such a structure. On the contrary, the place had been a positive hive of activity, which must surely have been dedicated to creating massive surpluses of both food stuffs and created objects that were not intended for use within the complex itself.

Further grand buildings had occupied the site, though placed beyond the boundary of the supposed palace itself, and a broad and well-paved road had led away from the complex in the direction of the nearby port. It was doubtless along this road that many of the objects created at Knossos and a large proportion of the food stuffs collected together there had been carried for shipment to other parts of the Mediterranean and beyond.

What staggered Evans and his contemporaries most regarding Knossos was just how skilled its builders had been. Not only had the original structures been light, airy and elegant, they were in many respects quite unique. For example, Crete lies in a region very susceptible to earthquakes. These are still frequently experienced across the region and there is strong evidence that even during its zenith, the building at Knossos had been seriously damaged by quakes. As a result, several departures from normal architectural methods had been employed, in order to make the structures as earthquake proof as possible.

Like later Greek architects, the Minoans had relied heavily on pillars to support some of their heaviest and most complex structures. The Minoan stonemasons had been experts at cutting and dressing limestone and yet on many occasions they had chosen to create pillars, not from stone but of wood. It is now estimated that such a technique owed nothing to ease of construction, but was in fact a safeguard. In some respects a stone column or pillar would be stronger than a similar-sized one created from the trunk of a tree, and yet in other ways it could be inferior. Wood has more 'give' and will bend and flex significantly – which of course is why trees don't fall down at the first sign of a strong wind or indeed an earthquake. It appears that the engineers at Knossos were well aware of this fact. In addition, stone columns will fall without warning, whereas wood may groan and creak for hours before it gives way. This is one of the reasons why miners have always favoured wooden pit props as against even metal ones and it was something the Minoan builders seem to have understood – probably as a result of long and sometimes bitter experience.

Dating both the building and its contents proved to be fearfully complicated. At the start of the early 20th century there was no process such as carbon dating, a technique that allows formerly organic remains to be fairly accurately placed in the historical timescale. Since nobody had even known that such an amazing culture had actually once existed, classification and dating had to begin from scratch. This might have been assisted by the fact that many examples of writing were discovered on tablets in and around the site, but unfortunately at the time there was no clue as to what the writing might mean. It would be decades before an interpretation of some of these carefully created documents would be achieved, although many are still as much of a puzzle to us now as they were to Arthur Evans.

Little by little Evans began to sort out his thousands of finds. He discovered that the many examples of pottery were especially useful because they could be divided into types and classifications, each of which indicated a different phase in the cultural development of inhabitants. Working carefully from the lowest layers, which he knew to be of Neolithic type because his excavations had been so careful, Evans could move forward in time, itemizing each innovation or change in style – right up until the final phase at Knossos, which he knew must have been well before classical times. He could tell, for example, that even just prior to its demise, the site at Knossos had been peopled by a bronze-using culture, but with absolutely no trace of iron. Since iron was being used extensively in Europe by around 800 BC, it stood to reason that the culture that created Knossos must be older than this date.

Using every scrap of evidence at his disposal, working right up until 1941, Evans gradually came to understand the length of time Minoan culture had endured – and roughly when it had come to an end. Obviously, advances in dating techniques have improved our understanding, which has also been assisted by the discovery and excavation of other 'palaces' and many other Minoan sites and settlements in other locations, most notably on the island of Santorini (also known as Thera), north of Crete. In the 1960s excavations began on Santorini under tons of accumulated volcanic ash in order to reach the former Minoan settlement that had been destroyed in a cataclysmic volcanic eruption around the 15th century BC. Since the disaster had struck quite quickly, the inhabitants had fled, leaving behind them a wealth of material that archaeologists are still excavating today. Further Minoan-type settlements have also been located in Sicily, southern Spain and even on the Mediterranean coast of the Levant.

In addition, references to the Minoans are included in records of the Ancient Egyptians, with whom the Minoans traded. Since dating of Egyptian history is now becoming much better understood, and because Egyptian wall paintings show Minoan pottery and objects that can be related to finds on Crete, knowledge of the differing periods in Minoan history is improving.

Finally, it is important to mention the name that has become attached to this culture. We have no idea what the Minoans actually called themselves, though we do have some references to what others, such as the Egyptians called them. This was certainly not 'Minoan' and in all probability such a character as Minos never actually existed. Evans used the name for pure convenience and wasn't the first person to do so. However, he was well aware of the mythological nature of the stories of King Minos. Partly in deference to the legends and mainly because he had to call his new-found culture by some convenient name, he was happy in the end to settle on the term Minoan, taken directly from the name of the famed king of Ovid's story.

Arthur Evans died in 1941, and though he had finished his personal excavations years before, he had never lost interest in the bright and utterly fascinating culture that he had patiently unearthed and catalogued amidst the brick-red soil of Crete. It is to this patient man that we owe so much of our present knowledge, whilst archaeology gained a great deal from his patient observation and scrupulous cataloguing. Although many of his methods would be frowned upon today, Arthur Evans still ranks as a seminal character in the establishment of true archaeology.

## Chapter 3

# The Colourful Culture

Over several centuries the modern Western world has come to rely heavily for its artistic, political and philosophical history on Ancient Greece. So strong has this reliance been that even experts in history sometimes tend to forget that this culture, no matter how fascinating and complex, did not spring, full blooded and complete, from obscurity. The mere fact that we refer to Greece as 'ancient' seems to infer that this is as far back in time as we need to look in order to understand at what point in time and from where anything worth referring to as 'civilization' originated. In reality nothing could be further from the truth.

The glory that was Ancient Greece began, by common consent, no earlier than around 800 BC. It was at this time that a series of recognizable city states began to emerge in the heartland of Greece. In the centuries that followed, these centres of population fought wars with each other, developed trade links, forged alliances and created written alphabets. Ultimately they were successful and rich enough to support an intellectual elite with sufficient time and resources to consider art, politics and even philosophy, rather than concerning themselves entirely with the simple necessities of survival.

Yet even the Ancient Greeks themselves, with their sumptuous architecture, complex political systems and reasoned thought, were quite well aware that they had achieved their own status only because they had stood on the backs of other, earlier people. The Ancient Greek historian Herodotus, who lived in the 5th century BC, travelled extensively beyond the Aegean. He was the first individual of whom we are aware who collected the material for his writings in a systematic way and who relied heavily on first-hand accounts from individuals whose own cultures differed markedly from those developing in Athens or Sparta.

Herodotus, who was born in what is modern Turkey, travelled to Egypt, and to Persia. Living at was then the crossroads of the known world, he was able to interview merchants and traders from far and wide, and he also had access to extensive libraries that contained the work of earlier, now forgotten, historians, as well as to the wealth of folk tales, legends and religious stories that proliferated in his time. His fascinating narrative, known as *The Histories*, shows time and again that the Ancient Greeks were well aware that their own civilization had been predated by a number of others, not least that of the Egyptians.

Priests in Egypt told Herodotus that their history already spanned many centuries and he saw at first hand magnificent temples and pyramids that had already been weathering away for centuries, built at a time when Greece was peopled by primitive barbarians who had come down in waves from the north as early as 1200 BC. Herodotus was left in no doubt that his own culture was a relative newcomer and, like many people of his time, he looked back to what he considered had once been a perfect European 'golden age' of which he and his contemporaries believed Ancient Greece itself was merely a pale reflection.

The Greeks at the time of Herodotus believed firmly that there had been several ages before their own that had been greater, grander and more perfect. In his poem, *Works and Days*, another Greek, Hesiod, who predated Herodotus by perhaps two centuries, talked of the 'five ages of man'. Hesiod was no historian in the modern sense, but he was dealing in subject matter that was fully understood by the thinkers of his day. Hesiod suggested that the first age of man had been a golden age. He wrote that, during the golden age, life for humanity had been perfect: mankind had lived close to the gods and it had not been necessary to work in order to have food and shelter. Hesiod suggested that during this long-lost period, people had remained young and vigorous, even after many decades and that humanity had been virtuous, peaceful and fulfilled.

According to Hesiod, a series of further ages had followed the golden age. The next ages had been those of silver and bronze. After these came what he called the heroic age, and finally the age of iron, in which he himself lived. In all of these successive ages, with perhaps the exception of the heroic age, Hesiod believed that humanity had degenerated and become less civilized than in previous ages. Nor was Hesiod alone in cataloguing the previous ages of humanity. The theme remained popular throughout the Ancient Greek era and was taken up by the much later Roman poet Ovid, who split the past of humanity into four ages and was as emphatic as Hesiod had been that humanity had not advanced.

Perhaps such an attitude isn't surprising. It seems to be the essence of human nature, even in our own era, to look back with nostalgia, even though when the past is studied dispassionately it can be categorically shown that, by almost every criterion available, humanity and civilization generally is advancing. Was this the case for Hesiod and other commentators of the Greek world? Perhaps, but it was not the total reason why Hesiod looked back towards a more settled and peaceful era. He knew, as did many of his contemporaries, that there was much about his own time and culture that was directly attributable to 'somewhere else'. This was especially true in terms of mythology and the ancestry of the Greek gods.

The Greeks had a sizeable pantheon of gods and goddesses, all of whom had a peculiar and changeable relationship with humanity. Undisputed ruler of the Greek pantheon in Hesiod's day was Zeus, a god of storms and thunder, who presided over an extended family of deities whose interpersonal relationships and history were complex and very confusing. The Greeks themselves knew and admitted that Zeus had not originated in their own homeland. Stories relating to Zeus indicated that he had originally come from the island of Crete, where the fables suggested he had been put for safety by his mother Rhea, against the tyrannical behaviour of his own father Cronos. It was on Crete that the Greeks believed Zeus had been nurtured to adulthood by a she-goat, before eventually overthrowing Cronos and taking command of the heavenly pantheon.

The more I looked at the Greeks, with their peculiar mindset, their atypical attitudes and their complex beliefs, the greater became my conviction that they were essentially correct and that they owed much to 'something else'. Whatever this something else was, it did not seem to be directly associated with contemporary cultures of the Ancient Greeks, such as the Egyptians, the Babylonians or the Persians. At the heart of Greek civilization, life and religion I could see the shadow of something that didn't appear to be particularly exotic but somehow uniquely European.

Not that Ancient Greece was immune from its contacts with the wider outside world. Many of the mathematical discoveries that were originally put down as uniquely Greek in origin turn out to have come from other places. Much of Greek scientific thinking almost certainly originated with the Sumerians in what is now Iraq, whilst elements of Greek geometry, although also reflecting Sumerian/Babylonian discoveries, were heavily affected by Egypt. All the same, something almost intangible developed in Ancient Greece that is not at all a reflection of either Sumer or Egypt. The Greeks adopted and maintained a passion for personal freedom – of both thought and action – that stood out sharply against the historical background of which they were a part. Independent thought prevailed in the groves and townships of the Greek city states, where the modern concept of democracy first tentatively took root.

Put succinctly, even the Greeks themselves believed that much of what they were had been inherited, and they sometimes looked south, beyond the Aegean Sea and into the Mediterranean to find it – specifically to that lovely island where Zeus was supposed to have spent his youth. All real knowledge of what Crete had once been appears to have been eradicated from the Greek mind in the centuries approaching the modern era, but there were echoes that reverberated around the marble hills and green valleys. Plato, the 4th-century-BC Greek philosopher carries the only surviving description of what the ancestor civilization of Greece may have been, though he actually describes it as being an enemy of Greece. He doesn't call it Crete, and he places it beyond the Pillars of Hercules, but, as we will presently see, Plato's description of the long-lost Atlantis and of its sudden and catastrophic destruction could only realistically be the half-forgotten story of Minoan Crete.

With more and more items from Minoan Crete being excavated from the deep-red soil of the island, and with new techniques becoming available to archaeologists, the comparisons between the Minoans and the Ancient Greeks is becoming increasingly unavoidable. Perhaps the only reason that the Ancient Greeks themselves were not fully aware of how much they owed to the Minoans was precisely because of the sudden and abrupt end of Minoan greatness, together with the circuitous route Minoan artistry, scientific accomplishment and religion took in order to heavily influence the Greek city states. The Crete that the Ancient Greeks actually did remember represented an island conquered and dominated by the warlike culture from Mycenae and practically all of what Minoan Crete actually had been had disappeared into the realms of myth, to become an aspect of the long-lost 'golden age'. Now, for the first time in nearly four thousand years, we can view the Minoans as they truly were – an independent and unique entity that represented Europe's first 'super culture' and a people who were more than partly responsible for laying down the foundations of what would one day become Western civilization.

Humanity had already arrived and was thriving in Crete as long as 130,000 years ago. Human tool users had somehow crossed the Mediterranean at this extremely remote period and were already making the most of the many opportunities this virtual Garden of Eden had to offer. This earliest group of Cretans probably died out or retreated during successive cold spells. It seems most likely that they had arrived by sea from the north coast of Africa and they are certainly not the people who would build the flourishing culture for which the island is now becoming so famous. For those individuals we probably need to look to a much later period, between 4000 and 3000 BC, by which time hunter-gatherers and then eventually subsistence farmers were present.

Where the direct ancestors of Minoan Crete originated remains a mystery. This is partly because no trace remains of the language spoken on Crete during the Minoan period. With the later incursion of the Greek Mycenaean culture, Crete's language gradually changed. This is known to be the case because the first form of Cretan writing has still not been deciphered, whereas the later Greek-influenced script is understood. Perhaps the Minoans shared a common heritage with the people who could become known as the Ancient Egyptians. Some historians see unavoidable parallels in terms of early Cretan hieroglyphics and there is a certain 'distant' resonance between Egyptian art and that of Minoan Crete. On the other hand, in many respects the Cretans seem to have had much in common with peoples inhabiting large areas of Western Europe during the Stone Age. The Minoans were great builders in stone – something that is evident throughout the islands of the Mediterranean, in southern Spain, France and especially up the western seaboard of Europe and into the British Isles – though of course the Egyptians were epic builders too.

Wherever the Stone Age population of Crete had originated, their naturally protected, fairly remote island home not only offered them security but also furnished them with everything they needed to live what must have been, even at that remote period, a fairly comfortable existence. Crete is one of the largest of the Mediterranean islands; it has an extensive coastline, which in the north at least has many natural harbours and beaches. As a result, the bounty of the sea has always had a great part to play in Cretan life. Although the island is generally mountainous and rocky, it has sizeable areas of rich, volcanic soil.

The first evidence for what could be called substantial communities comes from around 2800 BC and a fairly scant three centuries later, there is evidence that a flourishing civilization was developing.

From this period, for around a thousand years, archaeology offers a tantalizing glimpse into a culture that was quite unlike anything flourishing elsewhere at the time. It seems that from a quite early date the Minoans were capitalizing on any and all opportunities on offer in their island home. Exactly what the political structure may have been is still open to debate but, unlike contemporary cultures, such as that of the Sumerians, life in Minoan Crete was not based on powerful city states. Rather it seems to have been a place of relatively small settlements but with major regional centres that may be rightly or wrongly termed palaces, around which sizeable towns developed.

Throughout the whole period of Minoan Crete, no evidence has been found of a powerful elite or a monarchy; neither is there any indication at this period that the so-called palaces were fortified, either against attack from outside or from a rebellious populace. There is nothing to suggest that society on the island at this time was split along tribal lines. Relative isolation during the early years of the culture seems to have allowed a unique society to emerge and even when contact

44

with the outside world became the norm, the cohesion of the Minoan culture appears to have been maintained. Everything indicates a population ruled by consensus and not coercion.

Bronze came to Crete as early as 2700 BC and this means that the sailors of the island were already travelling significant distances because, although Crete flourished as a Bronze Age culture, the island itself did not possess the raw ingredients, copper and tin, needed to make the metal. As a result, a trading mentality developed early and the Minoans used the abundance of materials they did have to purchase the commodities they did not. Although Crete at this time had no perceptible standing army, it soon developed a formidable navy. Greek legends talk much about the Cretan's ability at shipbuilding and seafaring.

Archaeological finds show that trading from Crete during the Bronze Age was anything but a piecemeal affair. The 'palaces', the largest of which was centrally placed close to the north coast of the island, seem to have been places where local goods were collected and stored – perhaps partly as a bolster against times of want but much more likely to be traded on a larger scale. When Evans excavated Knossos he came across colossal clay vessels, which had once been used to store commodities such as olive oil, honey and probably wine. Can we assume that the smaller settlements on Crete were co-operating with the palaces to trade in a way that afforded 'economy of scale'? It seems likely, for one very important reason: even up to modern times, brides on Crete are often given presents of small, intricately carved seals made of stone. It has been considered for centuries that these seal stones bring good luck and that they will encourage young mothers to produce sufficient milk for their children, hence the Cretan name for the seals, which is 'milk stones'.

Many of the seal stones in question are extremely ancient. Archaeologists have discovered that such stones were used to impress wet clay, which when baked provided labels or tags for bundles of merchandise on or around the necks of jars. Many hundreds of different symbols are indicated on the seal stones. In other words, it looks as though there was more than an element of 'free enterprise' regarding the production of goods for both local use and for export. Seal stones are also found in Sumer and Babylon, but these often relate to royalty or powerful priesthoods, whereas in the case of the Minoans, ordinary individuals – perhaps small-scale farmers and artisans – seem to have used seal stones of their own, each sporting a personal or maybe a family crest.

Minoan Crete was surrounded by cultures that had also mastered the art of civilization and the Minoans cornered a market, not simply in agricultural produce but also in commodities that added to a successful and even an opulent life. Always artistic, Minoans were great producers of vibrant and sophisticated pottery. The kilns of Minoan Crete produced vessels with walls as thin as eggshell, superbly decorated and definitely meant more for show than for utility. This unique pottery found its way all over southern Europe, into the Middle East and down into Egypt. The artistry involved merely reflected the Minoan zest for life because the culture itself adorned its civic spaces and even the homes of its citizens with lively frescoes, of a sort that was not in any way derivative, but unique to the culture. Pottery was complemented by objects in silver and gold, beautifully crafted and traded far and wide, with examples having been unearthed as far away as southern Britain.

In addition to the luxury goods, many of which seem to have been created in workshops associated with the palace complexes, the staples of Minoan exports were fine wool, locally produced honey, olive oil, wine and finished bronze goods. Obviously anxious to exploit any and all opportunities for trade, the Minoans established outposts in southern Spain, Italy, down the coast of the Levant and were even mentioned regularly in Egyptian records. Lavish gifts were made to foreign powers, though probably not what could be termed as tribute because for many centuries Crete was safe from foreign domination, partly because of its own powerful navy but also on account of its remoteness.

The Minoans were also represented on a number of the islands in the southern Aegean. Indeed, the Minoan presence on the island of Santorini, 120 kilometres north of Crete, rivalled Minoan Crete itself. There the inhabitants lived an almost identical life to that enjoyed by their Cretan counterparts and, thanks to the disaster that eventually overtook the entire civilization, Santorini became a 'time capsule', from which so much about Minoan life has been learned.

The Minoans developed not one but several written languages. Initially, they communicated by way of hieroglyphics – not dissimilar to those of the Egyptians but nevertheless unique. It has not been possible to translate Minoan hieroglyphics because, unlike the case with the written Egyptian language, there has never been any Minoan equivalent of the Rosetta Stone. Without comparisons and bearing in mind that the Minoan spoken language is not known, these first efforts at written communication on the island and throughout its developing spheres of influence may remain forever a mystery.

With the passing of time a very different sort of written language also developed in Crete. It looks very similar to that known as Linear B, which was first deciphered by Michael

Ventris (1922–56), an English architect and language expert. Ventris showed that Linear B, a syllabic script containing around 87 components and found on Crete, was used to communicate Mycenaean Greek. The earlier form of the same written language is known as Linear A; it is thought to be closely related to the later Linear B but is descriptive of a language that is not understood. Whether this syllabic, linear script replaced the hieroglyphics in Crete is not known and it could be that the two systems of communication were used alongside each other, though for different purposes. It is possible that a decipherment of Linear A could furnish historians with a much better understanding of Minoan Crete, though even this isn't certain because in the case of the later Linear B script, most of the examples found deal with commodities, accounts and verification of transactions, rather than with literature.

The painstaking lifetime work of Arthur Evans provided the world with an intriguing glimpse of Minoan life. This has been supplemented by the findings on the island of Santorini, where a huge volcanic eruption, probably around 1450 BC, covered an entire Minoan settlement with ash, sealing it into a time capsule which is, even now, being rediscovered.

The Minoans were a gregarious, colourful people with a great zest for life. It is quite possible that the culture was essentially matriarchal and perhaps matrilineal. On the many frescos that have been found, as well as on pottery and in other artistic representations, women take a leading role. Women are shown wearing elaborate costumes, often with bared breasts over flounced skirts. Females are shown wearing elaborate hairstyles and headgear, whereas men are almost always portrayed wearing little more than a loincloth. Men are also frequently depicted in a stance that seems to indicate 'homage' to their more ostentatious female counterparts, with the back of a fisted hand pressed against the forehead.

Many experts, including the archaeologist Jacquetta Hawkes (1910–96) were of the opinion that the habit of Minoan art depicting men as inferior to women is born out of a deeply feminine-based religion, that they claim dominated Minoan society. It is suggested that the island was effectively run by dynasties of priestesses and that it was for them that the huge centres such as Knossos and Phaistos existed. The Minoans appear to have been devoted to a whole series of feminine deities, though it is likely that all of these reflect one great 'Earth Mother', who it would appear was worshiped across much of Stone Age Europe and parts of Asia from an extremely early date. Nearly all human forms depicted in European Stone Age art, across a huge area, are female. Perhaps, because of its geographical isolation, the goddess culture that had been so prevalent but which gradually gave way to masculine-based religion in the Bronze Age and Iron Age in the rest of Europe, perpetuated in Crete.

It is certainly possible to see reflections of this in later Greek religion. Although the Ancient Greek pantheon was dominated by gods, it still contained some very powerful goddesses, such as Demeter, that seem to have a long and illustrious heritage. Demeter became the centre of one of the most persuasive and perpetuating cults that immediately predated Christianity. The uniquely Egyptian goddess Isis eventually served a similar function in Western Europe and her worship also survived into the Christian era. Demeter and Isis may have represented race memories of the all-powerful goddess who had reigned supreme across vast areas prior to the rise of the patriarchal religions. It has even been suggested that the presence of powerful gods coincided with the advent of farming and that it was when hunter-gatherer existence ceased that the original 'Great Goddess' began to diminish in stature. If this is indeed the case, Minoan Crete clearly represented an exception to the rule because the Minoans were great farmers, and yet still perpetuated a goddess-centred religion.

The goddess of Minoan Crete was worshiped predominately in natural settings, such as mountain-top shrines and in caves. Many symbols are attributed to her but none have more significance than the famous double-headed axe, which was used everywhere as a good-luck token and as a votive offering. It is known that stylized double-headed axes also adorned the roof line of the palace of Knossos.

Knossos is by far the largest of the known Minoan structures, and it could be that it represented a deliberately created labyrinth that somehow aped the natural caves and settings where the goddess was worshiped. A sizeable portion of a hill was removed so that Knossos could be created. Knossos is located slightly inland from the present capital of Crete, Heraklion.

Knossos was not built in one phase but gradually grew to its eventual size between around 1700 and 1400 BC. When it was excavated by Arthur Evans, early in the 20th century, he was stunned by its dimensions. The palace contained literally hundreds of rooms and the fact that it was so large instantly dispels any notion that it existed purely to serve any monarchy or priesthood. Like all the known Minoan palaces it was built around a large, rectangular court – an open space where spectacles took place, with ample room provided for many hundreds of spectators.

Despite its many small rooms Knossos would have been light and airy. Only the outer rooms could have had windows or terraces but there were inner courts and many light wells, so that the sunlight could stream in from above. Walls were of stone but also ingeniously contained the previously mentioned wooden components that would 'give' under the duress of the frequent earthquakes that rock the region. Indeed, parts of the palace of Knossos were destroyed on several occasions, but never the whole structure.

The palaces of Minoan Crete were expertly created, by people who understood advanced techniques in architecture and building. Knossos was supplied with running water and complex sewage systems. In the throne room the chief priestess, either serving the goddess or actually 'representing' her, is thought to have officiated, but it is quite clear that Knossos, and the other palaces of Minoan Crete, were much more than places of worship. Rather, as we have seen, they appear to have been centres of commerce, places of manufacture, living quarters for artisans and administrators alike and storage depots for vast amounts of merchandise – much of which was probably destined for export.

Long after Arthur Evans packed up his tools and returned to Britain, a Canadian archaeologist and architect, J Walter Graham, made an extended visit to Crete. Graham was fascinated by Minoan building techniques and over a period of time took extensive measurements of the surviving foundations of the various palaces. He surprised himself by coming to the conclusion that the Minoans had used a standard unit of linear measurement in their building. He concluded that they had settled on a unit very similar to the modern foot, but slightly shorter at 30.36cm. Not everyone agreed with his conclusions but the world of archaeology was forced to concede that he must be correct when a previously unknown palace was unearthed at Zakro, in the very east of Crete. Its dimensions fitted perfectly with Graham's observations.

J Walter Graham's findings would prove pivotal to my own discoveries regarding Minoan culture because, together with the mysterious Phaistos Disc, the 'Minoan foot' led me on a journey that would eventually uncover the true worth of Minoan knowledge and accomplishment. What I discovered was the flowering of a genius that was unparalleled in the Bronze Age and which, in some respects, even eclipsed the genius of the Ancient Egyptians or the Babylonians.

*Chapter 4*

# The Great Traders

Even in these days of rapid travel by air, the Earth's oceans, seas and rivers represent a constant and busy highway. Huge container ports in almost all countries load and unload ships that constantly circumnavigate the world, carrying both crucial commodities and also merely desired luxuries from one continent to another. Of course there's nothing new about this, it is merely the scale of modern imports and exports that is staggering – as well as the range of merchandise being shipped. So reliant are we on international trade that in the past blockades have brought some nations to their knees. All parts of humanity rely absolutely on swapping what they do have for something they do not – something that has been going on for a very long time.

Historians a few decades ago were inclined to underestimate just how important trade was, even to our most ancient ancestors. As soon as hunter-gathering gave way to farming and communities remained in one area, a situation was certain to develop in which groups committed to a specific location would find themselves deficient in certain commodities. Since our species has always been quick to adapt to changing circumstances, it was inevitable that where a thing was needed, someone would find a way to supply it, and to earn a profit as a result.

A good example of a commodity that settled groups of farmers could not do without is salt. There are places well away from coastal areas where the farming potential is good. However, the daily need for salt, both for humans and livestock would have meant groups of individuals from inland areas regularly making what might be a long and arduous trek to the sea, there to spend days or weeks creating salt pans and evaporating sea water. Alternatively they could spend their days more productively at home and rely on a passing trader to supply the necessary mineral.

With a settled life sometimes came a degree of prosperity and the ability to grow more crops or to raise more livestock than was needed for a family or a group. As a result, trade in articles that were 'desired' rather than strictly needed also began to take place. We now know that even in these remote times a large number of people were constantly on the move, exchanging the goods that people either needed or coveted for items they themselves did not require or which they were producing specifically with trade in mind. One might live in an area rich in flint, from which all manner of tools could be made, even after the advent of farming and the arrival of the Bronze Age. A typical farmer in a flint-rich area could have spent much of his spare time, and his skill, turning out arrow heads or hand axes. These he would use to barter with passing traders, maybe for gold or silver jewellery, or for bronze implements he could not manufacture for himself. And so life continued, generation by generation, whilst isolated communities were able to obtain the goods they needed, thanks to these peripatetic merchants.

Despite the profit that was to be made in trading, moving items overland, especially large quantities of heavy goods, such as salt or flint, was time consuming, awkward and potentially dangerous. With the landscape of much of Europe being either bog, wasteland or thick forest, even from a very early date merchants and traders must surely have opted for water-borne travel when it was possible. Larger amounts of goods could be moved with ease by boat; there were no hills or even mountains to negotiate, no wild beasts to fend off and less chance of robbers who might cut out the middle man and steal your merchandise. Of course, travel by sea, even staying close to the coast, could itself be dangerous, but if the sailors had a good knowledge of tides and weather conditions, and if the journeys were undertaken in certain, predictable months of the year, the danger could be lessened, if not completely prevented.

Prior to around 4000 BC, boats were being used extensively, though in the main these were probably fairly small craft, used on rivers, marshes and perhaps in sheltered coastal waters. The problem with longer sea journeys did not lay with the bravery or competence of these early sailors, but in the technology at their disposal. The very first boats were almost certainly simply hollowed-out logs, or tiny craft made of a wooden framework covered in animal skin. Rafts of logs were doubtless also used, but none of these craft were suited to the rigours of offshore navigation. What is more, except in the case of a substantial raft, they would not be suited to moving sizeable cargos. A raft certainly could, but it is a craft for rivers and lakes and not at all suited to tidal conditions or squalls.

In order to regularly take a boat out of sight of land, and to create a craft large enough to carry a substantial cargo, it had to be made out of wooden planks. Even with all the ingenuity available, it would have been impossible to make a saw from flint, or any other rock, sufficiently accurate and sharp to cut a tree trunk into planks. Even when copper was first discovered and used, as useful as it might have been for some purposes, it was too soft to provide useful saws for wood. What was needed was a harder edge, and prior to the Bronze Age proper, that was achieved by adding arsenic to copper. This process offered the potential for a much sharper and long lasting 'edge' and it allowed trees to be cut into planks.

A great deal of ingenuity went into making the first boats that would have been useable and useful away from the safety of the most sheltered waters. In 1937, two brothers, Will and Ted Wright were walking along the shores of the River Humber estuary at Ferriby in East Yorkshire, England, when they saw some wooden planks sticking out from the river mud. What they had discovered turned out to have once been a sizeable boat, in fact one of three that were discovered in the same location. In more recent times the timbers of the boat have been carbon dated to around 1880 BC, which places the boat firmly in the Bronze Age. However, since it was of a very sophisticated design, it was probably very similar to wooden-plank boats that had already been made for quite some time.

A careful reconstruction showed that the first Ferriby boat had originally been well over 43 feet in length and 5.5 feet in width. It could once have accommodated 18 people rowing and could also have carried a significant cargo. The planks had been stitched together, using withies from the yew tree. The planks would have swollen eventually, but there would still be minute gaps between them and these had been carefully caulked with moss, over which had been laid strong oak laths.

This and its companions were boats suited to use in both river estuaries and coastal waters. Very similar shaped craft were still being produced on the east coast of Yorkshire in comparatively recent times. The only essential difference is that 'cobbles', as such boats are called in my native Yorkshire, have overlapping planks. These could be secured with iron nails, which were obviously not available to the Bronze Age sailors. As fishing boats they regularly dealt with the rigours of the North Sea, one of the most treacherous stretches of water anywhere. Such boats could easily have been taken across the English Channel and then down the coasts of France and Portugal, to enter the Mediterranean through the Pillars of Hercules.

It is therefore clear that the Minoan civilization, which was broadly contemporary with the Ferriby boats, could have built and sailed substantial sea-going boats to service their import and export needs. Indeed there is a fresco recovered from the island of Santorini that clearly shows Minoan boats with sails that could easily have carried cargo up and down the Mediterranean. In reality there could be no other answer. We know that exporting raw materials, such as wool, honey and olive oil, as well as importing the components of the Bronze Age culture of which they were a part, represented the lifeblood of Minoan civilization. This could not have been achieved without a sizeable merchant navy, together with armed ships to sweep the local seas clear of pirates.

One of the best ways of assessing just how far Minoan sailors travelled and traded is related to a particular metal, without which their culture could never have flourished in the way it did. The first metal to be used by humanity was copper. Although nowhere near as common as iron, which occurs at levels of 50,000 parts per million in the Earth's crust, copper is by no means the rarest of the metals, being found in quantities of approximately 70 parts per million. Copper certainly does not appear everywhere and there is little or none to be found on Crete, so even this first step in metallurgy had to be imported by the Minoans.

However, as early as 3000 BC, parts of the Aegean were being influenced by a trend in metallurgy that appears to have developed originally further east. This was the use of bronze. Although it can be worked fairly easily, copper on its own is an extremely soft metal and therefore of only limited use for making tools or weapons (unless arsenic is added). Copper can be sharpened to a keen edge but this will blunt extremely quickly – what was needed was a much harder metal. This was achieved by the addition of tin to the copper, though such an alloy could not be achieved until advances were made in the smelting of metals. Copper melts at around 1,085°C, so technology in the form of bellows was needed, together with charcoal, in order to bring copper to its liquid state, before adding tin. Prior to this, copper was often obtained directly from the ore, by means of heating and constant hammering.

The main problem for isolated cultures such as those on the islands of the Mediterranean was obtaining the raw material in the first place. This is especially true in the case of tin, which, at 2 parts per million, is only found in isolated locations. In Western Europe tin is to be found on the border of Germany and the Czech Republic (a source that was exploited early) and also in Spain and Portugal (though arguably this was not discovered until Roman times). Apart from extremely small amounts in Italy, there is only one other place where tin is readily available in Western Europe and this is the area of Devon and Cornwall, in south-west England.

There is at least some evidence that rather than struggling to obtain bronze for its own needs, Minoan Crete was actually exporting the metal to other locations. An oft-repeated symbol used in very early Minoan hieroglyphics is something that looks like the stretched hide of a sheep. What this actually represents, in a pictographic sense, is likely to be a bronze ingot. This shape for bronze ingots was extremely common all the way through the Bronze Age, and numerous examples have been found, specifically in early shipwrecks.

Bronze artifacts from Crete itself are extremely common and there was clearly no lack of the metal within the Minoan culture, so where were the Minoans obtaining the raw materials they needed – especially the tin – to fulfil not only domestic needs but to also furnish exports of the metal?

As we have seen, it is true that overland routes for all manner of objects and materials had existed across Europe right back into the Stone Age. Amber, from the Baltic, is regularly found in British burials from the period, whilst jet, a fossilized wood used for jewellery, which only occurs on the north-east coast of England, regularly found its way in the other direction. That's fine for such lightweight material, and in relatively small quantities, but the metal tin is extremely heavy and in those days, when there were no roads to speak of and when overland transportation of anything was both arduous and potentially dangerous, transportation of smelted tin or tin ore would have been difficult to say the least.

If the tin used by the Minoan civilization had come from the German–Czech border, it would have had a long and tortuous journey overland, even before it simply had to be shipped across part of the Mediterranean – hardly an ideal or likely situation for a culture that was creating more bronze than it needed. As already postulated, it is far more probable that Minoan Crete was obtaining both the copper and tin it needed by ship, direct from a location where it could be found close to the sea. That location could only have been the south-west coast of Britain, where both metals were found in abundance.

Not too far from the south coast of England, in the county of Wiltshire, stand the lonely ruins of the famed Stonehenge. This standing stone circle, which was commenced as early as 3000 BC, only received its largest and most impressive stones between 2000 BC and 1700 BC. If one stands, at the right time of day and at the right angle, it is possible to discern the ghost of carvings on two of these huge sarsen stones, as they are called. One of the carvings is of a very particular sort of dagger, whilst the other denotes what could only be a double-headed axe.

Both of these objects were recognized long ago as being representative of examples from the Aegean. Obviously, stone carvings cannot be accurately dated and whilst it was originally suggested that the carvings were Mycenaean, it wasn't long before experts were saying that since the Mycenaean culture of Greece did not arise until after 1600 BC, by which time Stonehenge had been abandoned, the carvings were unlikely to be of Mycenaean origin. However, this fails to address the fact that both of the carvings in question relate just as much to Minoan Crete as they do to Mycenae.

Over the last couple of centuries a number of objects have been found in high-status burials in the extreme south of England which are recognized to have been of Greek or pre-Greek origin. These include at least two gold cups, each of which closely resembled Minoan examples from elsewhere, and also ear adornments in the form of golden bees, which are also distinctly Minoan in form. The only reason these objects survived is because they had been buried and not retrieved until recent times. Since only a small proportion of precious objects in any civilization are normally found centuries later, it stands to reason that these were not isolated objects. Gold in particular is a metal that is constantly recycled, so finds of gold from prehistory are extremely rare.

Is there any evidence apart from this that the Minoan civilization enjoyed great success in its maritime endeavours? Indeed there is, because Crete is now known to have not only trading posts but also settlements in a number of different locations. Apart from smaller islands within the Mediterranean itself, Minoan settlements existed in Sicily, on the Italian mainland, in southern Spain and as far east as the coast of Palestine, as well is in North Africa. Nobody now doubts that Minoan sailors plied the Mediterranean from east to west and from north to south, as well as venturing into the Aegean. It is therefore not stretching imagination too much to suggest that the journeys went further, with Minoans passing out of the Mediterranean and into the Atlantic. Indeed, as we will presently see, there is great reason for believing that the cultural connections between Crete and southern England even involved a commonality of belief and knowledge never previously suspected.

Such journeys may seem to be epic by the standards of the period, but can be seen in a slightly more understandable light knowing that there was a Minoan presence in southern Spain, in association with a people known as the Los Millares culture.

With outposts in southern Spain it would have been possible to undertake trading journeys in stages. The sort of craft necessary to face the rigours of the Atlantic was not the same as the shallower-draught ships that could ply the Mediterranean. It is therefore likely that goods were trans-shipped, both on the outward and inward journey, via southern Spain.

A typical journey would have been from Heraklion in Crete to Sicily, thence perhaps to Sardinia, on to maybe Majorca and then south-west to Almeria. After that, a different form of craft would hug the southern coast of Spain before passing through the Pillars of Hercules and out into the Atlantic. It is extremely unlikely that the same crews would have been involved on all legs of this long journey, and not too much of it would have involved being out of sight of land. Copper in addition to tin may have been brought from England but the Los Millares culture had been smelting and fashioning copper from a very early age, so it is clear that large amounts of copper ore must have been available close by.

Of course, in the case of an island such as Crete, which has connections to all points of the compass, trade would also be taking place to the north, east and south. Probably the most important Minoan outpost on the northern route from Crete, up into the Aegean, was the volcanic island of Santorini, 120 kilometres north of Crete. It is now becoming obvious that Santorini (also known as Thera) was rather more than just an outpost of the Minoan Empire – it was a truly important location that stood at the civilization's heart.

How many people lived on Santorini during the Minoan period is hard to estimate, mainly because a great proportion of the former island simply ceased to exist when the volcano at its centre blew much of the surrounding land to pieces. This left what is known as a caldera, a torus-shaped crescent surrounding a central lagoon with a small and much more recent island at its centre.

Back in 1967, almost by accident, it was discovered that in one particular place on the island, and beneath many metres of consolidated volcanic ash, a settlement that had flourished just prior to the Bronze Age eruption still existed and that parts of it were in remarkable condition. Known as Akrotiri, it has gradually been excavated from its tephra covering, though much remains to be uncovered in the future. It turns out that Akrotiri was a thriving Minoan settlement, culturally and artistically almost identical with Minoan findings on Crete itself.

The part of Akrotiri so far exposed turns out to have been a prosperous and thriving town, filled with fairly luxurious houses. Unlike on Crete, where only foundations are likely to be uncovered from Minoan times, on Akrotiri there are extant walls up to three stories high, with rooms still carrying the paraphernalia of what appears to have been a comfortable and cultured people. Although no human remains have been found – indicating that the inhabitants had some warning of the great eruption and had left by sea, they seem to have abandoned their properties very quickly. Even the minutiae of life in Bronze Age times has been unearthed in Akrotiri, such as loaves of bread and a wealth of domestic objects.

Everything discovered indicates that the people on Santorini were definitely living the Bronze Age equivalent of the 'good life'. Interior walls of the houses were adorned with vibrant and colourful frescoes, of the sort that have also been discovered at Knossos and other sites in Greece. These depict various scenes from everyday life – a young boy carrying strings of freshly caught fish, beautiful young women presenting crocus flowers to what is probably a priestess, and pleasure boats sailing in the lagoon, with wonderfully adorned young ladies resting under sun shades.

Meanwhile, back in their town, the citizens revelled in well-organized streets and squares, good drainage and both hot and cold water supplied to most houses. The hot water was probably geothermal in origin and it is likely that in any case the island had more water prior to the eruption than is the case now.

The discovery and excavation of Akrotiri should have made it possible to date the major eruption of Santorini accurately; indeed, with the use of carbon dating, this has turned out to be the case. In the early stages of excavation it was noted that objects found on Santorini were not of strictly Minoan origin. This showed that trade was taking place across a sizeable area but it also offered another benefit. Since many of the objects in question could be placed within a historical context, for example on mainland Greece or islands such as Cyprus, archaeologists estimated the eruption to have taken place around 1450 BC. Meanwhile, more recent and more accurate carbon-dating evidence from Santorini puts the disaster closer to around 1620 BC. It is also known that the world went through a significant 'climatic event' at this time and tree-ring dating, which can be the most accurate of all, would assert that the eruption actually took place in 1628 BC.

Akrotiri is a true time capsule, like the city of Pompeii in Italy, though from a much earlier period. It remains to be seen what other evidence will be brought to light as further excavations are undertaken. What is of great interest is that the discoveries at Akrotiri do much to rescue the reputation of Sir Arthur Evans. He was often accused of over-romanticizing the Minoan civilization and his reconstructions at Knossos were also accused of owing more, in an architectural sense to the art deco style that prevailed during his era than it did to true Minoan building styles. Akrotiri demonstrates that, if anything, Evans understated the glory of Minoan civilization and life, whilst the reconstructions he supervised turn out to have been extremely accurate.

Students of Minoan culture can indeed be grateful that the caprices of one of the largest volcanic eruptions to take place during human history managed to 'preserve' as well as to destroy, for had it not been for the way the eruption happened on that fateful day in 1628 BC, all the remarkable evidence left on this bright and still truly beautiful island may have been destroyed completely.

## Chapter 5

# The Seeds of Tragedy

It is almost certain that the island of Santorini lay abandoned and deserted on that fateful day around 1628 BC. Perhaps a few reluctantly abandoned domestic animals wandered around, hungry and nervous at the constant tremors that shook the island by day and night. It is likely that wisps of acrid smoke were already rising from the centre of the old caldera but it had been the earthquakes, one after another, for many days that had finally convinced the population that the time had come to go.

Geologists and historians alike, when talking of the disaster, fail to mention the logistical nightmare that would have attended the removal of several thousand people from this fairly isolated rock. We are, after all, talking about the Bronze Age, and, as efficient and numerous as the Minoan navy might have been, it must have taken many trips to fully abandon Akrotiri and its many satellite settlements. However, since no evidence of human remains has been found during the half century since Akrotiri was rediscovered, it appears that the majority of people had fled. The only other grizzly possibility is that the entire population, or a major part of it, was huddled together in some spot that ceased to exist in a horrific split second as the volcano blew itself to pieces.

It is inappropriate to say that there is a volcano on the island of Santorini, as we might in the case of Iceland or New Zealand. Rather the island itself is a volcano. Fire-breathing mountains like this one are the great saviours but also sometimes the slayers of life. Volcanoes bring metals and minerals to the surface from deep within the earth. In so doing they release the very chemicals upon which all life depends in order to exist and flourish. They operate on a geological time scale, sometimes slumbering for many centuries before suddenly bursting into ferocious and cataclysmic life. Certainly nobody living on Santorini during the 15th century BC had experienced the anger of their own volcano, or even understood that they were clinging to the uppermost reaches of its underwater mass. They may have periodically experienced tremors, as the mountain breathed and groaned, but they could never have been aware of what was taking place below the beautiful, sheltered lagoon, where we know they spent their leisure in pleasure boats, and where ships from the merchant fleet found safe anchor, even in the stormiest months of the year.

After the last eruption before Minoan times, the crater had become filled with lava, which had quickly solidified in the cool water of the Mediterranean. This had eventually formed a plug, like someone pushing a cork into the spout of a simmering kettle. But the forces that had created the volcano in the first place had not ceased. On the contrary, slowly but surely pressure was building below, as yet more super-heated magma sought to find its way out. The result was all too inevitable. After what would seem to humanity to be a long period of time, but was barely the blink of an eye in the life of the Earth, the force exerted from below became greater than the downward pressure of the solidified rock.

Finally, the whole accumulated mass, including the plug of rock that extended down into the volcano's mouth, could no longer restrain the irresistible force. The accumulated energy was not simply large enough to split the plug asunder and send the cork flying out of the kettle's spout – the whole event was far more spectacular than that. The blast did not simply 'move' the plug, rather it instantly pulverized it into the finest of dust. This was an explosion that would have made any of the nuclear weapons we have managed to produce seem like a party cracker in comparison. Upwards of 40 cubic kilometres of pulverized rock was instantly blown high into the air, with a colossal bang.

Sound travels relatively slowly in comparison to light, so people tilling their fields or out on the sea fishing, many hundreds of kilometres away, would have first been aware of the most tremendous flash. Day or night, the brightness would have eclipsed the brightest sunlight but none of the many thousands of individuals who were aware of it would have had the remotest idea what was taking place.

Depending on their distance form Santorini, the already terrified people would have soon experienced a low rumbling, followed by an ear-splitting roar, so intense that it would have deafened anyone close by. The ground hundreds of kilometres away would have shaken, and no doubt masonry began to topple 120 kilometres away on the northern shores of Crete. However, this was merely the start of the disaster.

Not all the material surrounding the volcano's crater would have been thrown into the air. Much of it would have immediately collapsed back into the sea, causing a great displacement of water that would spawn tsunamis, spreading out from the island to all points of the compass. Whilst at sea, the waves would have been relatively harmless. Only when they reached the coastal shelves of other land masses would the water begin to build up to create the irrepressible wall of water with which the world is presently familiar after the recent disasters in the Far East. People on the Aegean islands to the north, and on the Greek mainland, those in the Egyptian delta and on the North African coast must all have been affected. The resultant, almost instant, death toll from the tsunamis can only be guessed at, but it must have amounted to tens of thousands.

Long term, the Santorini eruption would probably have killed ten times as many people. So much fine dust, thrown high into the atmosphere, would cause huge and long-lasting changes in weather patterns. There are reports from far-away China from this period that talk about fierce weather and non-existent harvests – and this was the only culture that left a written record of the event. Ice cores from remote Greenland also indicate a period of worldwide disruption to weather patterns, all of which may ultimately have led to many hundreds of thousands of additional deaths indirectly attributable to this one eruption. Most of those who experienced a long and lingering demise, caused by the failure of crops upon which they relied absolutely, would have no idea what was killing them. With the hindsight that modern knowledge allows us, however, there can be no doubt that the explosion of the volcano on Santorini represented one of the greatest disasters ever to strike humanity.

Things could hardly have turned out worse than they did for Crete. Most of the populous settlements and certainly the majority of good, sheltered harbours were and are on the northern coast of the island – the coast immediately facing Santorini. Rocked by the attendant earthquakes, devastated by the relentless, massive tsunami, northern Crete then suffered even more as the larger remnants of the pulverized volcanic ash began to fall back to Earth. We can imagine that, for many of Santorini's inhabitants, doubtless evacuated to Crete, the terrifying ordeal they had already undergone was merely a precursor to an inevitable death, under tons of falling masonry or fathoms of seething water. And for those who did survive, perhaps years of hunger, disease and misery lay before them.

What must have made matters infinitely worse was the fact that Minoan Crete had spawned a large population. Although the island could grow its own food, much of the land would have been temporarily ruined by the accumulation of metres of ash. It is a paradox that the very substance that ultimately makes the soil of Crete so fertile can be, initially, a violent killer. Seedlings are choked and the chemical composition of the ash requires months or years of weathering to release its life-giving ingredients. Along much of this coast of Crete, the mountains rise steeply from the narrow coastal belt, so that if any knowledge of the forthcoming tsunami had been present, plenty of people could have quickly climbed high enough to escape its initial force. But when the water finally subsided, practically everything upon which they relied would have been utterly destroyed.

Every ship at harbour in northern Crete would surely have been dashed to pieces in a moment. It takes decades to create a merchant navy, and with many of the sailors almost certainly killed at the same time, who was to crew new vessels, even if circumstances had allowed them to be built?

There is evidence of this cataclysm in just about every area of Minoan Crete that has fallen under the trowels of archaeologists. The Palace of Knossos was badly damaged, despite the fact that it stands well above the harbour that served it. Ceilings collapsed, walls fell and much of the accumulated wealth and the vast stores contained within the structure must have been utterly lost.

It also has to be remembered that this was a period in history long before a modern scientific or logical approach to explaining the event was possible. After such a disaster even we would be flocking to the ruins of our churches to seek solace in prayer, but to the European Bronze Age mind, an occurrence such as this would immediately have been seen as godly retribution. This was a superstitious time. People in the eastern Mediterranean were quite familiar with earthquakes, which fell under the province of a deity the later classical Greeks knew as Poseidon – the 'earth shaker'. There is evidence that, like many of the later gods, Poseidon had come originally from Minoan Crete. Those present must have reasoned that they had somehow incurred the wrath of this most terrible agency, to cause him to be so very angry. What had been wrong with their devotions? How had they managed to make one of their most important deities so furious? Evidence has even been found of human sacrifice taking place in northern Crete in the immediate aftermath of the devastation – something for which there is no sign from any earlier period. The fact is that, faced with the wrath of Gods, people anywhere will go to extraordinary lengths in order to re-establish the status quo; from what little we know of Minoan Crete after Santorini, the whole civilization was, at least temporarily, in meltdown.

Archaeology is not really the same thing as catalogued history. Its resources and methods are improving dramatically, year on year, but it is still primarily the study of the way people lived and not an accurate diary of events. Only the written word adequately explains specific happenings and although Minoans at the time were definitely writing, much of what they have tried to tell us remains a mystery. This is primarily because we cannot read the script known as Linear A, examples of which have been found in the palaces and elsewhere on the island. The problem is one of language: since it is not known where the Minoans originally came from, or what language group they belonged to, unless some reference between Linear A and another known language is forthcoming, as was the case with Egyptian hieroglyphics and the Rosetta Stone, we will remain forever ignorant of what the Minoan scribes had to say.

Later Minoan script, which is known as Linear B, has been deciphered, since the language used on Crete by that time was akin to archaic Greek. But most of the clay tablets found prove to be nothing more that tallies of commodities and lists of various sorts. These are useful enough, but they are not narratives and tell us nothing about the hopes, aspirations or religious beliefs of the people, let alone offering a catalogue of historical events.

I hope to show in due course that there were broad, cultural similarities between many of the peoples inhabiting Western Europe in these remote times – even those peoples living as far away as the islands of Britain. Twenty years of tireless research have brought me to understand that these were all very sophisticated cultures, which were highly numerate and extremely bright. However, their history, culture and religion, like much of their astronomical and mathematical knowledge, were deliberately passed on orally. These were cultures dependent on memory and the spoken word, whose priests could spend decades meticulously memorizing everything that was important to their tribes and their world. When such a chain of carefully maintained and flawlessly transmitted information is broken, all that remains are the story-cycles, which once served as aide-memoire and through which priceless and timeless truths were safeguarded.

If the Minoans really were as similar to the Ancient Britons and other cultures in the West as I am certain they were, we may never find written evidence of the sort that has taught us so much about Sumer, Babylon or Egypt. Under such circumstances we can simply take what archaeology is able to offer, and also look deeply at the oral traditions that span not only decades, but many centuries. If we are very careful and learn to read the messages that definitely do survive, we can not only learn a great deal more about the colourful and vibrant people of Bronze Age Crete, but also begin to understand what inspired closely related people living across a vast area of Europe prior to the massive cultural changes that took place in the years after Santorini but before the rise of Ancient Greece.

The disaster that was Santorini came at a pivotal time in the ascent of humanity in the region – or did it merely lead to a massive displacement, the effects of which would be felt for many centuries? Certainly, post-Santorini, things began to change markedly in the region. More warlike and martial peoples were starting to spread south into the Aegean from further north. It is possible that some of these had been displaced by the aftermath of the eruption and the devastation it brought not only to farmers, but to the remnants of hunter-gatherer and nomadic pastoral communities from less organized and civilized areas. It isn't simply farming that is momentarily floored by a worldwide catastrophe. Nature as a whole suffers from even the temporary breakdown of normal weather patterns caused by massive eruptions. The whole food chain is affected, with the result that the larger prey species of humans undergoes a slump in population. This in turn displaces whole tribes, who set out to find areas where food is available – even if they have to steal it from farmers who are somehow managing to get by. Farming depends upon storage – laying up grain and other food stuffs against more difficult times. Such an accumulation would look very attractive to starving hunters or pastoralists and they would ultimately be quite happy to fight to possess it – in turn displacing peoples who may have been settled and civilized for generations.

# A Region in Flux

It is impossible to determine absolutely that the changes that began to take place within Minoan society after around 1600 BC can be attributed directly to the Santorini eruption. Maybe what came about was the result of a whole series of events, some or all of which were unrelated. What is certain is that not long after the Santorini eruption, sudden and quite dramatic changes are registered in the archaeological record of Minoan Crete. Foremost amongst these is a realization that the rule of the Minoan elite, which was formerly invested totally in Knossos and the other so-called Cretan 'palaces', passed not only to a different group of people but also to individuals from outside of the island altogether. The familiar if unintelligible

Linear A script gave way to another, Linear B; although looking similar to Linear A, it can be understood, since the language upon which the Linear B script is based is archaic Greek.

The documents make it clear that although Minoan Crete was still broadly autonomous, it had fallen under the somewhat oppressive yoke of a culture from some distance away. In order to understand how this had come about, it is necessary to take a look at what was happening across the wider area at this stage of the Bronze Age.

As far as truly ancient prehistory is concerned, little is known of the inhabitants of the greater part of Greece in terms of their language or ethnic origins. Right back to about 7000 BC, human communities were already inhabiting areas of Greece. These people, who may originally have been hunter-gatherers and then pastoralists and farmers, began to live a settled life, often in heavily fortified areas – which could indicate a tribal and perhaps a warlike mentality or may simply have been a response to invaders coming into the area from further afield. These people, like most of those to the west of Greece and across all of Western Europe, spoke languages that were broadly unrelated to the modern Indo-European family of languages. They represented much of the population of Western Europe during the Stone Age and the first part of the Bronze Age. It is elements of these peoples that grew to become the Minoan culture of Crete and its outposts.

Now there occurred a massive event, of which history actually knows very little except its results. During the Bronze Age a very different people began to migrate out of the Steppes of Central Asia. These people were nomadic pastoralists, who drove their herds of livestock across vast areas, looking for suitable grazing. This was a way of life that had predominated for countless centuries with little change. However, something happened that created one of the most pivotal human migrations the world has ever known.

Around 2000 BC, groups of these Asian nomads began to spread south, into Anatolia, also known as Asia Minor. Some of them went on to create the great Hittite Empire, a truly warlike society that conquered Babylon and even threatened Ancient Egypt. After a few centuries in Asia Minor, other groups of these people, who are broadly referred to as Indo-Europeans, moved down into the body of Greece, displacing or intermarrying with the people who already lived in the area. Certainly there was a transformation because it was at this time that the language families that are the origins for most modern languages in Europe, Asia Minor, parts of Central Asia and India started to predominate.

The Indo-Europeans were extremely successful, most probably because they were so warlike. Eventually they pushed across the whole body of Europe. This was a sea change as the more aggressive culture gained the ascendant. There are strong indications further west that the Stone Age and the start of the Bronze Age had been a fairly peaceful time in Western Europe (as it clearly was in Crete). No doubt disputes and skirmishes did take place, but the Stone Age people of the area appeared to have no policy of military expansion and may all have been of similar racial and linguistic backgrounds.

In fact elements of this original language group still survive in remote areas. The Basques of Spain and France are a good example. Now restricted to north-western Spain and south-western France, the Basque language is quite unrelated to the Indo-European languages that surround it. How this could have happened, without being a historical language that already existed when the Indo-Europeans arrived, is difficult to understand. That is why most linguists accept it as being a truly ancient historical remnant of a language group that may have been spoken across much of Europe at one time. The German linguist Theo Vennemann claims there is more than enough evidence to suggest that Basque is indeed the remnant of a language group that existed across much, if not all, of Europe prior to the arrival of the Indo-European languages.

Since in non-literate cultures no trace of a spoken language can be found in the archaeological record, experts are left with piecing together modern languages at their most basic level, in order to try and tease out clues as to their origins and interrelationships. This can be a fearfully complicated, deeply academic and very time-consuming quest, without any certainty of arriving at a consensus with which peer experts will agree. My own opinion is unequivocal: I see so many similarities in the way cultures at either end of the Mediterranean viewed astronomy, mathematics, measuring systems and almost certainly religion too, prior to the Indo-European watershed, that I have no doubt these cultures were closely related, both culturally and in terms of their almost constant contact with one with another. I appreciate this goes against the once generally held theory that people in the Stone Age and Bronze Age lived a fairly static existence but as I have already pointed out, it is becoming increasingly obvious that people actually travelled a great deal. How much easier that would have been if similar or virtually identical languages existed across the whole area and if cultural and religious affiliations were also broadly similar.

The study of genetics, which is progressing at an unprecedented rate, has allowed the DNA of living individuals

77

to be checked, in order to be able to show their ancestors' migrations. At the same time archaeological specimens, particularly skeletal material, can also be analysed. In addition to DNA information, which may or may not have survived, samples can now be extracted that indicate where an individual was born and raised, judged by the chemical fingerprint of bone and teeth, due to the water they drank early in life. The results are surprising in that they show people in the Stone Age and early Bronze Age travelling across significant distances. These moves are not necessarily associated with the shift of an entire culture, but that of one or a few individuals.

Many examples have been found of individuals or families that may have been raised in, say, what is now Switzerland, only to end their days in southern England. These are not random examples and since any archaeological record represents only a small sample of the state of affairs in any particular era, finding even a few cases of people who have travelled long distances tends to infer statistically that it was quite common. The totality of the evidence says to me that if people moved about so regularly, across what are now considered to be national boundaries, at such an early date, they were not being impeded from doing do on the grounds of race, tribe or nationalistic considerations. As a result, we can at least infer that people all across Western Europe and beyond had a great deal in common and probably spoke more or less the same language.

It is only the massive success of the Indo-European incursions across Europe that has eclipsed so much of what went before. No doubt languages similar to Basque were once spoken in other regions. With the success of the Indo-Europeans, original language groups became more and more marginalized, until most disappeared altogether. The probable reason Basque survived is a testimony to the geographical nature of the areas where the Basques ultimately found themselves. They eventually lived in very mountainous, remote places, which probably had little commercial value to the newcomers and which were, in any case, more easily defended.

In addition, there are some quite hidden aspects of the pre-Indo-European languages to be found in the far west of Europe, apart from Basque itself. The clue is hidden not so much in words but in the syntax of certain languages, most especially Welsh and Gaelic. Although both these languages use mostly borrowed Indo-European words, their structure is different from most modern European languages and certainly owes 'something' to extremely ancient and possibly uniquely European roots, which, in the opinion of some experts in ancient linguistics, may go back as far as 45,000 years,

Whether the incursion of these new peoples from further east always represented conquests is in some doubt. For example, from around 2000 BC the British archaeological record starts to feature new types of pottery and more advanced metal-working techniques. Few experts doubt that there was an influx of new arrivals at this time, creating a culture in Britain known as the 'Beaker people'. With few signs of widespread warfare or violence from the period, it is quite possible that the Beaker people were willingly assimilated into the ancient Neolithic culture of the islands. Unfortunately, although new and unique forms of pottery and better tools and weapons can survive to be found by archaeologists, changes in language or even religious practices remain invisible.

What few doubt is that the period from around 2000 BC onwards formed a watershed as far as the population of much of Europe was concerned. In many areas the Stone Age and the start of the Bronze Age appear to have been relatively peaceful. Certainly in Britain there are hints of a settled existence. As time went on, there is more evidence of local aggression, indicating a stronger clan or tribal structure. Whereas early burial mounds contained the remains of every class of society, it appears that a more 'warrior-based' culture emerged, in which clan chiefs were buried surrounded by weaponry and personal adornments. Old sites of ritual and religious significance, such as, for example, Stonehenge, were gradually abandoned, whilst fights over territory and resources seem to have been much more common.

Something broadly similar was taking place much further east, in Greece. More warlike and aggressive peoples were spreading down through the mainland from the north and east. The original inhabitants were either conquered, assimilated into the new cultures or were pushed ever further west. Other original inhabitants were safe for a while, since they inhabited islands such as Crete, which would have been difficult to assault, bearing in mind the broad swathes of sea that separated them from the mainland. Crete in particular was so isolated and had such an efficient navy and civil infrastructure that – had it not been for the disaster that was Santorini – it might well have survived much longer than it did. But the truth seems to have been that it was severely weakened, leaving itself open to the avaricious gaze of the Indo-Europeans, looking out from their new territories in Greece; and the most aggressive and successful of these peoples was the Mycenaeans.

*Chapter 6*

# The Mysterious Disc

Well away from the prosperous and busy northern shore of Minoan Crete, south of Knossos and across the mountain passes, lay another of the Minoan palaces, which today is known by the name of Phaistos. The palace here guarded a significant valley and appears to have been somewhat more fortified than other examples at Knossos, Malia and Zakro. Phaistos was built at one of the relatively few spots on the Cretan south coast with safe anchorage and good harbour facilities.

It is known from archaeological digs that took place at the start of the 20th century that, like its contemporary palace at Knossos, Phaistos was regularly damaged and even more or less destroyed by earthquakes (probably three times in successive centuries), and there seems to be little indication that it was ever extensively rebuilt after the Santorini eruption. No examples of Linear B writing have been found at the site and it does not appear to have had a part to play in the Minoan/Mycenaean period. The area was repopulated during the Iron Age and this new township was probably ultimately destroyed as a result of its citizens being involved in a battle with a nearby province.

Like the other Minoan palaces Phaistos was a range of buildings surrounding a large, open courtyard. It was never as large as Knossos and, perhaps for this reason, it has always been considered to have been of provincial importance. Nevertheless, the Palace of Phaistos did safeguard one treasure of immense significance. It was found in 1908 by an Italian archaeologist named Luigi Pernier, in the basement of a building in the north range of the palace. This incredible artifact, which lay protected by the rubble above it for upwards of three thousand years, is known today as the Phaistos Disc.

The Phaistos Disc is made from fired clay. In other words it was not simply left out in the Sun to dry, but had been carefully prepared in a kiln. It was found in an almost undamaged state and has proved to be a great puzzle, from the moment it came to light right up to the present day.

The Phaistos Disc is somewhat larger than a modern CD/DVD disc, at about 15cm (5.9in) in diameter. Both of its sides are covered with hieroglyphic characters, set within incised spirals and divided into groups by incised lines crossing the spirals. It is clear that the disc was very carefully created and there seems little doubt that the various hieroglyphics must have existed as dies or seals, most likely individually carved onto stone. These were pressed into the wet clay of the disc, creating the images we see today. The incised spirals and connecting lines were obviously created by hand after the hieroglyphics had been applied.

What makes the Phaistos Disc all the more mysterious is the fact that although clay tablets with hieroglyphic characters very similar to the ones it carries have been found in other parts of Crete, nobody has the slightest idea what they might mean. The more usual written language of Minoan Crete was a deliberately created script, composed of individual letters, not unlike a modern alphabet. This comes in two forms. The first is Linear A, which has never been deciphered, and Linear B, which being based on archaic Greek is now understood. The hieroglyphics used on the Phaistos Disc and found elsewhere on Crete bear no similarity either to Linear A or Linear B. At first sight they might be mistaken for Ancient Egyptian hieroglyphics, though no correspondence has actually been found.

*A reconstruction of side A of the Phaistos Disc.*

*A reconstruction of side B of the Phaistos Disc.*

Each hieroglyph could represent a concept, a word or even a phonetic sound. The pictures are mostly naturalistic in composition, representing people, boats, fish, various plants, shields, weapons and unknown objects. Although identical hieroglyphs appear on both sides of the disc, there is not the same number of them and neither do they appear in the same order.

It appears from the locations at which examples of the Minoan hieroglyphic script have been found elsewhere in Crete that their use overlapped that of Linear A, so perhaps they were never intended to serve the same general purpose in terms of listing merchandise or cataloguing stores of goods, which is what Linear A (like the later Linear B) was most likely used for.

As with Linear A, the main problem present when trying to decipher what the hieroglyphs mean lies in the fact that the original Minoan language is not known. Neither have any documents been found in which Minoan hieroglyphs were used alongside an understood script. Examples of the hieroglyphics appear to predate the use of Linear B, by which time their meaning could have been lost or their use simply abandoned.

The Phaistos Disc represents one of the greatest historical puzzles of all time. Search the internet or specialist bookshops and you will find dozens of claims from individuals that they have at last managed to work out what the disc says. Over the years I have carefully looked at as many of these supposed interpretations as possible, but none of them, either from academics or gifted amateurs, is in the least convincing – how could any of them be when the Minoan tongue is lost to us, probably for all time?

My first knowledge of the Phaistos Disc came nearly 30 years ago, on the first day of a holiday I was taking in Crete. I saw a facsimile of the disc in the window of a souvenir shop and was instantly drawn to its strange characters and odd patterns. I soon acquired a copy of the disc, which I still possess and which stands on my desk as I write these words. Every spare moment when I wasn't travelling around the island on that first trip to Crete was spent staring at the disc – and for a very good reason. From the first moment I had seen the disc, it spoke to me. From the outset, this could not be in words, since I am as ignorant as anyone regarding the Minoan language; I am no expert in ancient writing or derelict tongues. The language in which the disc spoke to me was one of mathematics. From the outset I turned my attention not to what the hieroglyphs might 'say', but rather what they could 'do'.

Almost since childhood I have been utterly fascinated by both astronomy and calendars. Where this predisposition came from I have no idea. Even as a small child I would often be found, late at night, staring out of my bedroom window at a clear, winter night sky. In those days people from my background rarely dreamed of striving for an academic career, such as astronomy, so I became an engineer. My love of the stars stayed with me, though, along with the allied fascination for the measurement of the passage of time.

Since I was also obsessed with ancient history, I quite naturally made myself acquainted with the methods our distant ancestors had used to measure the passing years and their knowledge of the relationship of time to the starry patterns they saw above their heads. I learned how important it had been, especially to early farmers, to be able to know precisely how long the year was, so they could judge the most crucial times for planting crops and other tasks associated with the land. I knew how the first genius civilization, that of the Ancient Sumerians, had split their year, both theoretically and actually, and I made myself familiar with the truly unique method of measuring time that developed along the Nile in Ancient Egypt.

It could be that this rather unusual interest, which had occupied me for as long as I could remember, was why the Phaistos Disc almost instantly spoke to me in a way that it may not have done to an expert in linguistics. Not being remotely conversant with the 'meaning' of the hieroglyphs, rather I noticed the patterns they formed on both sides of the disc, and the number of symbols there were in each group, throughout the spirals. What seemed apparent to me, because of my earlier experience, was that the Phaistos Disc was definitely meant to represent a calendar of some sort.

Many months of both frustration and joy followed as I tried to understand how the symbols on the disc, and their distribution, related to passing years. Little by little, the disc began to reveal its secrets, leading me to gradually realize that in front of me was one of the most sophisticated devices ever created by humanity. The Phaistos Disc was and is a multi-functioning device with which it is possible to keep track of Earth's irregular year and also to monitor the movements of the Sun, Moon and the inner planets of the solar system with stunning accuracy.

For readers who wish to fully understand not only what the Phaistos Disc can do, but how it achieves its remarkable feats, please see Appendix One. To me, the nuts and bolts of the disc's many functions are the greatest fascination of all, but not everyone has my love of simple numbers, so within the chapters of this book I have tried to keep these to a minimum.

The basic problem with which all early farmers were faced was quite simple, but somewhat difficult to address. What we judge as being a year is actually the time it takes the Earth to orbit the Sun once. Because of the angle of the Earth relative to the Sun, during this orbit the Earth undergoes 'seasons' – times at which either the northern or the southern hemisphere experiences the heat of summer and the fierce cold of winter. For anyone wishing to grow crops, it is essential to understand the way the seasons work. Plant crops too early and they may be destroyed by cold and damp; plant them too late and they might not have the time to mature before the cold of winter sets in again. In many geographical areas the window of opportunity is quite small – with possible famine and a lingering death being the result for the historical farmer who got it wrong.

This would not be too much of a problem if the Earth year resolved to an even number of days. Unfortunately this is not the case. The true length of the Earth year is just over 365.25 days. This is a number that cannot be easily split into smaller components, such as months or weeks and so it was natural to round off the year, often to 365 days, so that it could be more easily split. But if no compensation is made for the extra fraction of a day beyond 365 days, the pattern of weeks and months that has been established will begin to 'drift' throughout the yearly cycle. All too soon the months that formerly represented spring will be occurring in summer; seeds will be sown at the wrong time and disaster will follow.

In our own very literate and numerate culture we deal with the situation in a somewhat 'cranky' but generally effective way. Our method of reconciling the true year with a fairly regular civil calendar is to treat the year as if it consisted of 365 full days. This period we split, someone irregularly, into 12 months. Of course the true year is not 365 days in length, so we have to make compensations. The method we use is a modified version of a system dreamed up by the Ancient Romans. Every four years, we call the year a 'leap year' and add an extra day to the civil year, which becomes 29 February. This expedient is not quite enough to keep things right, so we have another rule that we apply. If the leap year coincides with a century year, such as the year 1900, we do not add an extra day in February, whereas if a leap year coincides with a millennium year, such as 2000, we do add the day.

These rules keep things more or less right in the longer term and the civil year is rarely at odds with the true year by more than a day in any given year. One of the main problems with this system, and because of historical tampering, is that our months are not all equal. As children we have to remember the little rhyme:

'Thirty days hath September, April June and November. All the rest have 31, except February clear, which has 28 and 29 each leap year.' Though as we have seen, even these rules have provisos.

Going back into the mists of time, our ancient ancestors had a variety of different ways of rectifying the true solar year into a useable and generally understood civil calendar, none of which were particularly effective and many of which required constant tinkering to keep them reasonably accurate.

To the Sumerians, who inhabited the Fertile Crescent between the rivers Tigris and Euphrates from around 3000 BC, the problem was as much one of 'tidiness', as well as the potential difficulty faced by farmers. The Sumerians could count and write very well, and those who comprised the Sumerian civil service had extremely ordered minds. Different methods were employed at different times but the main way that the Sumerians regulated the year was by starting out with a theoretical year of 360 days, divided into 12 equal months. Of course 360 days is well short of the real year, so the Sumerian scribes allowed the inaccuracy to continue until the civil calendar was 30 days or so adrift from the solar year. At such times they added an extra month to the year by royal decree. This generally happened every six years and more or less took care of the immediate problem, but it still meant the calendar was wrong by just over half a day every 6 years, a discrepancy that would itself accumulate and eventually lead to another 'one-off' correction.

Fortunately the Sumerians were very good astronomers and were able to judge the true length of the year. Theirs was an autocratic society and the populace simply followed whatever instruction came from above. With changes made when necessary the Sumerians seemed to have managed the problem effectively, if somewhat erratically. What really mattered to the scrupulously pedantic Sumerian scribes was that a 360-day year was tidy and that it conformed to the civilization's base-60 counting system.

The other major civilization at the time that Sumer was building itself into a powerful and cohesive society was that of the Ancient Egyptians. Despite enduring for far longer than any other historical civilization managed to do, Egyptian mathematicians never chose to complicate matters more than was strictly necessary. For thousands of years Egypt celebrated a year of 360 days, with five extra days added as holidays. This left the shortfall of 0.25 days a year that quickly accumulated. To most farming cultures working on the scale that Egypt did, this would have become a real problem, but to the Egyptians the true length of the year was not really an issue.

Because of its geographical location, it rarely rains in Egypt. From first to last the culture was utterly dependent on the great river Nile, along the banks of which the civilization flourished. Once a year torrential rain thousands of kilometres to the south, captured in the headwaters of the Nile, caused the river to flood. This flood eventually reached Egypt, where the Nile overflowed its banks, watering the fields on either side and replenishing them with a layer of rich silt that was brought down by the river.

The Egyptians judged the timing of the inundation of the Nile by way of an astronomical event, which took place each year. They literally religiously watched the behaviour of the brightest star in our skies – Sirius. For some weeks each year, when seen from Egypt, Sirius could not be seen, because it rose in the glare of the Sun. Eventually, thanks to the changing position and angle of the Earth relative to the Sun, Sirius rose once more, before the Sun at dawn. This event is known as the helical rising of Sirius and it was the prompt to the Egyptians to be ready for the Nile flood. It was an event that was treated as being quite separate to the months of the calendar, which slipped hopelessly throughout the year over a protracted period of time. However, since Sirius was the prompt Egyptian farmers needed, everything could be calculated from the yearly date of its helical rising.

When the Ancient Roman civilization came along, it relied for its calendar on models from further east. The emperor Julius Caesar (100–44 BC), realizing that an accurate year was necessary, but had not yet been achievable by his reign, employed the best astronomers and mathematicians to calculate how the year could be put right and then regulated. The result is known to us as the Julian calendar. The system devised was similar to the one we use today but unfortunately the people on whom Caesar relied got things slightly wrong, with the result that by the 16th century the civil calendar was once again hopelessly out of step with the solar calendar.

It took a pope, someone with the power to affect not one but most countries in the West, to finally put things right. The pope in question was Gregory XIII (r. 1572–85). Like Caesar,

Gregory employed the best brains of his time and then gave instructions to Western Christendom to make the appropriate changes. Most Catholic countries did so immediately, although the Protestant states took a long time to come into line. In Britain and much of its empire it did not happen until 1752, by which time ten days had to be removed from the calendar in order to get things working properly. Riots followed, in which the less well-educated people complained that ten days were being stolen from their lives.

Cultures far from Europe had their own ways of dealing with the measurement of time, and some of these were radically different to the European models. Central and South American cultures, prior to the arrival there of Europeans, had excellent astronomers. Instead of attempting to regulate the solar year to a civil year directly, the Central and South American model involved a whole sequence of different, interlocking calendars, measuring the cycles of the Sun and Moon, as well as those of other planets such as Venus. Instructions regarding planting and harvesting at any given time were doubtless handed down to the populace from above, since the civil calendars in use spanned many years and were fiercely complicated.

A perfect procedure to solve the problems caused by such an unco-operative year would be to decide upon a length for the civil year, and then to compensate for its inaccuracy by adding or removing a day at 'exactly' the time it was necessary to do so, rather than at the end of a year. However, this would appear to be far from easy, whilst still maintaining a fixed and fully understood civil calendar. The first message the Phaistos Disc taught me was how this could be achieved, and indeed *had* been achieved by the brilliant Minoans.

First and foremost, the Minoans settled for a civil year of 366 days. This meant immediately that they would eventually be removing days from the calendar and not adding them as we do. The Phaistos Disc showed me that the Minoans had celebrated 12 months to the year and that these alternated between 30 and 31 days. In addition, they also kept a different calendar count of 123 days, which ran alongside the civil year. After 4 cycles of the 123-day calendar – 492 days – one day was removed from the civil calendar, whatever that date happened to be. It was as if the day had never existed. With this one very simple procedure, the Minoan calendar would have remained absolutely accurate for upwards of five thousand years before any additional change would have been necessary.

It has always caused me to laugh out loud whenever anyone subsequently suggested that this method of compensation was not a Minoan invention, but had been thought up by me. Not only is it possible to demonstrate how the system worked, using the Phaistos Disc, but I could never, in ten lifetimes, have thought up anything nearly so simple and yet so incredibly accurate. In fact I am somewhat flattered that anyone might assume I could have done so.

The magical period of 123 days is not related to any external happening. It is an intellectual calendar, which exists to regulate the civil calendar but which also contributes to a host of other feats which the number systems used on the Phaistos Disc can allow anyone to perform.

What makes matters even more startling is the fact that the Phaistos Disc can assist in compensating, not simply for one sort of year, but for two. It might sound strange to suggest that there is more than one sort of Earth year, but the length of the year really depends on how one looks at things. To understand the difference between the two major sorts of Earth year, tropical and sidereal, I refer interested readers to Appendix Two. For those who are willing to accept my word, a tropical year is 365.2422 days in length, whilst a sidereal year comprises 365.2564 days. Only a culture that had a deep understanding of astronomy and planetary motion would ever discriminate between these two types of year, and yet the number bases of the Phaistos Disc make it possible to compute either sort of year with absolute precision.

Side A of the disc contains 123 characters, whilst side B has 119 characters. This unique choice allows for two additional calendar counts. First there is the 123-day count I have already mentioned; then there is a 119 day count. If the 123-day count is used, compensations are made for the sidereal year, whereas if the 119-day count is used, compensations are made for the tropical year (for details see Appendix One).

Over a long period of research it gradually became apparent to me that the choice of correction calendars, comprising cycles of 119 and 123 days, had actually been a stroke of genius and that these choices had been allied to a deep understanding on the part of the Minoans of astronomy, as well as a working knowledge of geometry.

Most ancient cultures were fascinated by the skies that appeared to turn above their heads. The star-spangled heavens were considered to be the domain of the gods and were often venerated as such. To the creative mind of humanity, many of the stars appeared to form patterns which were memorable. These patterns, or constellations, became, in the minds of the watchers, fearsome animals, brave heroes, beautiful women and even domestic utensils. It was useful as well as fanciful to be able to recognize and name star patterns, because it represented the start of being able to understand how the heavens moved.

The way we see the stars from any point on the Earth's surface, apart from the equator, changes seasonally, as the Earth moves on its yearly journey and its angle changes relative to the Sun. Because the stars are so very far away, the basic patterns formed by the groups of stars change very little, even over vast periods of time. All that alters seasonally is the times they rise in the east and set in the west and the height they climb above the horizon. However, there are other heavenly bodies that do move independently of the stars. One of these is the Sun, which effectively doesn't move at all but appears to do so because of the turning Earth and the Earth's orbit. Another is the Moon, which is Earth's satellite and so is revolving around us. The other heavenly bodies that have independent movement are the planets of the solar system, five of which can be seen with the naked eye. Like the Earth, the planets are revolving around the Sun. They look very much like bright stars, but they shine for a very different reason. Whilst distant stars – which are all suns, many of them very similar to our own – shine as a result of the light they emit, the planets shine because they reflect light from our own Sun.

All the planets of the solar system orbit the Sun in more or less the same plane, but at different distances from the Sun. Some, like little Mercury, which is closest to the Sun, have orbits that are extremely short, whilst others are much further out and take many years to pass once around the Sun. However, as far as we are concerned on Earth, the Sun, Moon and the planets all seem to take the same path across the sky, which is known as the 'plane of the ecliptic'.

It is useful to think of the sky as being like a stage on which a play is performed. The stars and other distant objects in space represent the backcloth and scenery on the stage, whilst the Sun, Moon and the planets might be said to be the actors on the stage, who move independently of the scenery.

In order to know where a particular planet is at any given point in time, it was useful to our ancient ancestors (and of course to us) to split the path they follow into more or less equal units. In most cases this was 12 (mainly because there are 12 full-Moon-to-full-Moon cycles in each Earth year, which occur in different parts of the sky in turn). Each of these sections became known because of the pictures that seemed to be formed by the background stars. These sections of heaven are often referred to as the signs of the zodiac.

Not every culture settled on 12 signs of the zodiac and not all split the sky in this way at all, but most did – many learning from each other as trade, travel and even conquest spread ideas around the ancient world. As far as our own present zodiac is concerned, it was usually considered to be ultimately of Sumerian origin but great doubt has been cast on this theory thanks to the work of two past professors from Glasgow University in Scotland. Some decades ago Professors Michael Ovenden and Archie Roy set out to discover where our current zodiac originated. Using a combination of some fairly obscure Ancient Greek poetry and their peerless knowledge of the way astronomy functions, Ovenden and Roy came to the conclusion that what we might call the 'modern' zodiac, must have come into being sometime around 2000 BC and that it must also have happened at roughly 30° to 35° north of the equator. It became obvious to Ovenden and Roy that there was only one culture that fitted the bill, this being the Minoan culture on Crete.

Meanwhile, the Sumerians had a zodiac of their own, which also contained 12 constellations or zodiac signs. It is generally suggested that the Sumerians, again with their tidy minds, chose to split this great circle of heaven into 360 units, which ultimately became known as degrees. Thus, during each month of the 12 month year, the Sun would pass across 30° of the zodiac, which on Earth was roughly equivalent to one month.

It will come as no surprise to the reader that out of this fascination for the heavens, geometry came about. Just as the sky was considered to be comprised of 360 units or degrees, so circles here on Earth could be split in the same way, which eventually made all sorts of mathematical problems easier to solve.

It all makes eminent sense. Maybe the Sumerians opted for a 360-day year because they had already chosen to split the great circle of the sky into 360 units, or perhaps it was the other way round, but one thing was certain: a year of 365.25 days or even one of 365 days would have made for a very complicated and almost unusable form of geometry. The sky may not have been totally logical in its choice of numbers, but the Sumerians definitely were.

The only real problem with this way of looking at things is that no matter how tidy it may appear to be, it isn't strictly correct. When seen from the Earth, it is obvious that the Sun moves through the zodiac by 1/365.2564th part of the zodiac on any given day and this is not 1/360th. The difference isn't much but it does make astronomical calculations fiercely difficult if one wishes to be totally accurate. Nevertheless, it suited the Sumerians, and also to a lesser extent the Egyptians. However, what the Phaistos Disc eventually taught me was that the Minoans, and most certainly other cultures during the European Bronze Age, had not settled on either a year of 360 days or 360° in a circle.

It all depends on astronomy and geometry being the same thing, and just as surely as the Minoans celebrated a civil year of 366 days, for which they cleverly compensated, they also considered circles to be comprised of 366°. Of course this sounds odd to us, but it was actually a very useable system, and it had the advantage of being much closer to the truth as far as astronomy was concerned.

Once again, I don't expect readers to take my word for this. The proof of my findings lies in the appendices to this book, which any reader can check for his or herself. But the fact is that the number sequences on which the Phaistos Disc is based, in addition to indicating how to keep the yearly calendar working properly, can also be used as an extremely accurate way for working out the position of the Sun, the Moon and the planets Mercury and Venus within the zodiac, at any time of any day – ever.

Why would the Minoans want or need to do this? The answer is quite straightforward. The Minoans were, first and foremost peerless sailors, who travelled far and wide on their trading expeditions. Good seamanship in the open ocean demands an excellent understanding of the sky and the way it works. All ancient cultures that took to the water steered their ships by the stars, and the better one understood the workings of the heavens, the less likely one was to come to grief.

By this point in my research, alarm bells were beginning to ring in my mind. This was because of a culture far from Crete, in the windswept islands of Britain. Together with a colleague, Christopher Knight, I had embarked on a quest regarding truly Ancient Britons and their knowledge, which would make the Minoans and their world so much easier to understand.

## Chapter 7

# Measure for Measure

Perhaps it is an inevitable aspect of the way education works across the generations, but it is a fact that anything discovered today about history is likely to take a full generation or sometimes more before it starts to be taught to students in school or college. Beyond this 'time lag' there are occasions when even irrefutable evidence is ignored by historians, who tend to be a conservative bunch on the whole. This is especially true if such evidence crosses disciplines. We live in a world in which specialization is seen as being both desirable and necessary. Though understandable, this situation is also sometimes lamentable, particularly if it means that old and worn-out paradigms perpetuate much longer than they should.

Historical researchers such as myself, who are not tied to the academic wheel, are sometimes able to recognize things orthodox historians do not and this often comes about because we have different backgrounds and skills that committed academics do not. This was definitely the case with regard to my study of the Phaistos Disc, which relied as much on my background as an engineer as on my knowledge of the Minoans.

It was my knowledge of engineering, and the mathematics that go with it, allied to my interest since childhood in astronomy that caused me to view aspects of ancient history in a very different way. I am not alone in this regard and so it was probably quite natural I should take up the sword on behalf of another engineer with astronomical interests.

The true genius of Minoan knowledge only became apparent to me thanks to research I was also undertaking into the stone-shifting or 'Megalithic' cultures of Stone Age and Bronze Age Britain.

It all came about because of the lifelong work of a man named Alexander Thom (1894–1985). Thom was, for many years, Professor of Engineering at Oxford University. He had been born and raised in Scotland, the son of a farmer. Like me, Thom had been fascinated by astronomy from early childhood. In addition, he had a love of sailing the sea lochs and coasts of his native Scotland and these two interests, quite outside of his eventual chosen career, furnished him with a quest that would span many decades.

On his many early sailing expeditions, Alexander Thom became quite familiar with the many standing stone circles and avenues that dot the Scottish landscape – many of them overlooking lochs or the ocean. Little was known about these structures, which are to be found in a great arc across the far west of Europe, but especially in Scotland, England and Ireland. The people who had left these often giant epitaphs from as early as around 3000 BC had gone to great trouble to create them. Stones had been sourced, and then often brought miles to be erected in elaborate patterns. It was generally thought around the time that Thom was growing up that the motivation for all this effort had been primarily religious or cultural, but Thom subsequently had his doubts.

With his knowledge of astronomy and his love of seamanship, Thom wondered if the Scottish standing stone circles, most of which were created during the late Stone Age or early Bronze Age, had been some sort of astronomical devices, used for ascertaining the fiercely complicated patterns created by the Moon across long periods of time. He reasoned that knowledge of these patterns would have been invaluable to the people of the time. Undoubtedly they had been sailors, because getting around the wastes and forests of Scotland at this very early date would have been fiercely difficult, whereas the sea and the lochs offered unparalleled opportunities for both fishing and commerce. In addition, the west of Scotland in particular is a land of many islands, which could only be accessed from the mainland and from each other by boat.

Using what spare time was at his disposal, together with his rapidly growing engineering and mathematical knowledge, Thom embarked on a quest that would span most of his life. One by one, he began to meticulously measure and survey all the major stone circles and stone avenues in Scotland, England, Wales and parts of France. He was eventually able to prove to the majority of those who had an interest in the Megalithic cultures (Megalithic simply means 'big stone') that many of the circles and avenues had indeed been created with observations of not only the Moon, but also the Sun and planets in mind. Thom became the acknowledged father of a new form of archaeology, which to this day is known as astro-archaeology, since it deals with the fascination our ancient ancestors had for the heavens.

Perhaps unfortunately for him, Alexander Thom made another discovery regarding the stone structures of Ancient Britain and France that was less willingly taken on board by his peers. He could not avoid noticing that strange patterns were beginning to emerge in his meticulously obtained measurements. It all too soon became obvious that there was an underlying similarity in most of the sites that indicated a common linear unit of measurement had been used in their construction.

What made matters worse was that the unit in question was not something general and variable, such as the length of a man's foot or that of his forearm, but rather was exactly the same, wherever Thom found it – to an extent that no matter how strange it seemed it was obvious that our Stone Age and Bronze Age ancestors had been using a carefully defined unit.

In those days of imperial measurement, Thom defined this unit, which he christened the 'Megalithic yard', as being 2.722ft in length (82.966cm). It never varied, from site to site, by more than a tiny amount and so, statistically, this proves that the measurement was correct.

Archaeologists are not generally mathematicians or astronomers, but they are not stupid either. It immediately occurred to some of them that Thom's Megalithic yard had to be nonsense. This was because they could see no way in which a really accurate unit of linear measurement could have been passed, intact, across many thousands of square miles of land, over a period of at least two thousand years, without changing in the slightest. How could such a unit have been maintained? No matter how these early farmers had tried to define the measurement, with lengths of hemp or wood, the caprices of a damp climate and the inevitable mistakes made by those in charge of the unit, would have seen it vary across time and distance. In any case, how could different tribal groups at such an early stage in history have been expected to co-operate to the extent necessary to preserve the unit?

Thom could not answer these questions. He checked and rechecked his calculations, only to discover that there was nothing whatsoever wrong with them. Indeed, he was awarded a specially struck gold medal by the British Statistical Society, which applauded his super-accurate surveying and number crunching. Sadly, in the end this meant nothing. Archaeology had its carefully protected paradigms regarding ancient history, and it wasn't about to have its world turned upside down by an engineer. Alexander Thom was ridiculed during his life, and despite our best efforts across two decades of additional proofs of his work, his findings are still not accepted by mainstream archaeology today.

It seemed to me, as a fellow engineer, that there was nothing at all wrong with Thom's findings. I even measured some of the sites in question myself and came up with identical results. Certainly I could see that the findings might prove to be uncomfortable in the safe and secure world of the historian and the archaeologist, but this was surely no reason for ignoring something that was self-evidently true, no matter how awkward it might also be?

There seemed to be only one way forward if Thom's reputation was to be salvaged. Together with a colleague and fellow writer, Christopher Knight, I embarked on a search for the reality of the Megalithic yard. In our minds, it was a reality – because unlike the archaeologists we were willing to note the irrefutable evidence. All that remained was to ascertain where the unit came from and how it was transmitted so accurately, across such a great area and through so many centuries.

After weeks of thinking and exchanging ideas, we became convinced that the only way of fixing such an unchanging unit, without recourse to exotic metals for making actual measures that could be handed on across generations, was to rely on something that never changed, but which could be checked whenever it proved to be necessary. This turned out to be the spinning Earth and the regular patterns of the sky.

The Megalithic yard had been created wherever and whenever it was needed, using a few wooden stakes, a piece of twine with a weight on its end, and an observation of the planet Venus. In addition a simple but quite essential procedure was necessary, but this could easily be passed on by word of mouth, probably through a perpetuating priesthood; as long as it was followed, the results would never vary.

What it comes down to is this. Venus, during a particular part of its cycle when seen from Earth, was observed passing across a gap in a carefully constructed braced wooden frame which was equal to 1/366th of the horizon, whilst a simple pendulum was allowed to swing back and forth. If the pendulum swung 366 times during the passage of Venus across this gap, the length of the pendulum *had to be* exactly half of a Megalithic yard. Since Thom had shown that half of a Megalithic yard had been used frequently on the Megalithic sites, it seemed more than reasonable to suspect that this had been the original unit and that it was doubled simply for the sake of convenience.

This procedure works because, during this part of its cycle as seen from Earth, Venus moves at a known and constant speed. It also works because a pendulum of any given length will always swing back and forth in the same period of time, irrespective of how gently or vigorously it is swung. In other words, as long as the simple rules are observed, the resulting measure will always be the same, wherever in Britain or France the procedure is employed. Strictly speaking, the length of the pendulum does vary by an incredibly small amount, because the force of gravity acting on the pendulum differs by a tiny proportion according to the latitude at which the experiment is carried out. This leads to a very small discrepancy in the size of the Megalithic yard between the north of Scotland and Brittany in France. Such a tiny variance is fully in accord with Thom's suggested deviation in the size of the observed Megalithic yard.

This could surely be the only answer for the reality of the Megalithic yard and in two cases during the procedure, the number 366 is apparent. More pointedly, it would soon become obvious that our Megalithic ancestors had been familiar with geometry of the same 366° variety that had been used in Minoan Crete.

What I obviously needed to do at this point was to see if there was any evidence of the Megalithic yard having been used by the Minoans. If there was, there would be strong evidence of common units of measure and even geometry being used across a huge geographical distance at a very remote period. Although this seemed unlikely, it was the case that the Minoan civilization was flourishing at the same time as many of these giant stones were being lifted into place in Britain, and there were even carvings on some of the giant sarsen stones of Stonehenge that could easily have been Minoan in origin. In addition, as I suggested earlier, it is almost certain that the tin the Minoans needed for their flourishing bronze industry came from south-west England.

When it came to establishing units of measurement used by the Minoans I was lucky in that a Canadian archaeologist by the name of J Walter Graham had looked closely at this very issue during the 1960s and 1970s. Carefully measuring the sites at Knossos, Phaistos and Malia, Graham came to the conclusion that the Minoans had used a common unit of measure. At first this looked very different from the Megalithic yard, because Graham declared it to be 30.365cm in length – very similar to, but not identical with, the modern statute foot. Graham initially had his detractors, probably for the same reasons Alexander Thom had been disbelieved, but in the end his findings were proved by the subsequent discovery of a previously unknown Minoan palace at Zakro, in the far east of Crete. When Graham measured this site he discovered that it conformed exactly to his previous findings, so there could no longer be any doubt that the unit he called the Minoan foot had been a reality.

But how could this unit have had anything to do with the much longer Megalithic yard? Not only did it prove to be connected, but the very connection gave me a better insight into how the degrees of the 366° system had been further broken down into smaller units. These days we split degrees of arc into 60 minutes of arc and minutes of arc into 60 smaller seconds of arc. It turned out that Megalithic geometry was similar, but not identical. It didn't take me long to reason that 366 Megalithic yards and 1,000 Minoan feet were exactly the same thing. This particular unit of length, equal to a modern 303.65 metres, was very special.

If the polar circumference of the Earth was split into 366 units, or degrees, each unit would measure 109.31 kilometres. Should we then choose to split each degree into 60 Megalithic minutes of arc, each would measure 1.8219 kilometres. If we now split this – not into 60, but 6 further units, which we call

Megalithic seconds of arc, the result would be 303.65 metres. This measure is exactly equal to 366 Megalithic yards and also 1,000 Minoan feet!

What did this tell us? Well firstly it demonstrated that the whole Megalithic measuring system was, almost unbelievably, based on a very accurate assessment of the polar circumference of the Earth. But it also demonstrated admirably that 366 Megalithic yards and 1,000 Minoan feet were the same length and represented 1 Megalithic second of the Earth's polar circumference.

Perhaps the Minoans had found a unit as long as the Megalithic yard to be unwieldy for the sort of buildings they were creating. Who could say at this distance in time? However, what was absolutely clear was that the Minoans and the Megalithic peoples of the far west of Europe used the same form of geometry and had measuring systems that were based on the size of the Earth. What was more, their smallest units of linear length were intimately related.

No trace of a written language from the British Stone Age or Bronze Age has ever been discovered and in all probability such a thing did not exist. We know from the much later Celtic culture in Britain that there was a tradition for knowledge to be passed on orally, even though, in the case of the Celtic priests, known as Druids, the acquisition of such knowledge could take 20 years! The whole Megalithic system of measurement, with its attendant linear units and its ability to measure time with as much ease as it measures distance, mass and volume, lends itself very well to oral transmission. The truly stunning fact about this system is that it never splits a number. Everything is achieved, from beginning to end, with simple whole numbers and yet, in its abilities and its symmetry across geometry, distance and time, it is far superior to the measuring systems we use today.

Knowing just how amazing human memory can be if it is programmed in the right way, I would not be in the least surprised to imagine that a British Megalithic priest, trained from an early age, could carry everything he ever needed to know about the measuring system in his head.

Clearly this does not seem to have been the case in Crete, otherwise why would the Phaistos Disc exist? The most likely explanation is that because of its location, its natural resources and the cohesion of its population, the Minoans went beyond the sort of co-operation possible in far-off, cold, windswept Britain. As a result they had become a genuine civilization in the modern understanding of the word – and an evolving form of written communication is one of the attributes generally associated with a thriving civilization. It is therefore likely that the Minoan priesthood arrived at a stage where it became possible to commit their knowledge, or parts of it, to the written word. All the same, this is unlikely to have been common because nothing else like the Phaistos Disc has ever been found on Crete, Santorini or any of the other suspected Minoan outposts.

At first it seemed reasonable to wonder whether this ingenious system of measurement and the knowledge of astronomy that funded it might have been brought to the shores of Britain by the Minoan tin traders, but it soon became obvious that this could not be the case. Long before the Megalithic peoples of Britain and France had been hauling great stones into place, they had been building structures that predated the stone circles and avenues. These are the circular ditches and banks known as henges. There are still many henges to be found, some of which are extremely large. In my own area of Yorkshire in the north of England there are a series of henges, each of which is so large it could easily accommodate the largest gothic cathedral. Christopher Knight and myself were able to demonstrate that these henges had also been constructed using the Megalithic yard – and more to the point, units of 366 Megalithic yards, which amply demonstrate the underlying geometry.

These giant henges were created as early as 3500 BC, at a time long before the people of Crete had aspired to anything that could be termed a civilization. By a logical process this suggests that if there was any cross-fertilization of ideas, it had to have travelled, not from east to west, but the other way. A much more likely answer is that the Megalithic system of measurements was endemic to the original inhabitants of Western Europe – or at any rate to far-flung cultures within that particular group of human beings. It certainly existed long before the Indo-European peoples began to migrate into Western Europe and it seems likely that it was their presence and influence that eventually caused it to be eclipsed and, to a great extent, abandoned.

With the Indo-European influx, cultural influences began to shift. Early Indo-European cultures, such as that of the Hittites, had contact with the civilizations in the Fertile Crescent and in Egypt. These civilizations were using a different form of geometry, and different linear units. The influence of these cultures moved west with the Indo-Europeans. As we shall see, particularly in Ancient Greece, the acceptance of a geometry containing 360° became the norm. Since the developing Western world ultimately looked towards Ancient Greece as its inspiration, the form of geometry that presently predominates across the globe is of ultimately Sumerian origin and owes little to the genius of the earlier inhabitants of Western Europe.

From around 2000 BC, the Phaistos Disc lay forgotten, but protected, below the ruins of a once-great Minoan palace. The genius to which it pointed was eclipsed, but the same was certainly not true of the civilization that had created it. Historians still generally accept that the Minoan civilization was superseded by that of the Mycenaeans, from the Greek mainland, but the true story is infinitely more complex than a total conquest.

## Chapter 8

# Kings in Gold Masks

All that can be said for certain regarding the Minoan civilization during the post-Santorini eruption is that it somehow fell under the subjugation of a culture that was rapidly gaining ground on the mainland of Greece. The people concerned are known to us as Mycenaeans, after their hill-top capital of Mycenae, in north-eastern Argolis, in the Peloponnese, southern Greece.

Such was the subsequent vigour with which successive Mycenaean rulers tore down earlier edifices and towns, to replace them with more-modern and ever-more-secure examples, that almost any trace of the development of the culture long since disappeared. In fact the whole arrival of Mycenaean culture remains something of a mystery. Doubtless they represented a branch of the Indo-European peoples, originally from the Steppes of Central Asia, that had migrated west and south. It is probable that whatever culture they encountered across much of the Peloponnese presented weak opposition and the Mycenaeans appear to have been fully in charge of large parts of the area by the time of the Santorini eruption.

This is a difficult period for historians, since Mycenae was so heavily affected by its contacts with Minoan Crete that it is difficult, if not impossible, to know how these connections came about. Some experts still assert that, following the Santorini catastrophe, warlike people from the Peloponnese were able to invade Crete. This is possible, because large areas of mainland Greece were probably more or less sheltered from the worst effects of the eruption, whilst Crete and its navy had been dreadfully ravaged. Others think this scenario is less likely and suggest that the much-damaged Minoan culture may have willingly formed a partnership with the northerners. The Minoans may have had outposts or settlements in the area, there could have been dynastic marriages or confederations of some sort that were already in place prior to Santorini, or other scenarios could equally have been possible.

What is not in doubt is that, ultimately, the Minoan culture was subsumed by that of the Mycenaeans – though only in part. This is obvious because the language originally spoken by the Minoans was soon abandoned. As I have pointed out, Linear A inscriptions found in Crete have never been deciphered – indicating that the language being spoken was not of the Indo-European family. Subsequent texts, in Linear B, are now understood. The form of writing is similar, if not identical, and is undoubtedly a Minoan invention, but it eventually became applied to archaic Greek, which is an Indo-European language.

It is obvious that Mycenaean culture was run very differently to that of the pre-Mycenaean Minoans. There are many examples to prove this is the case. With the exception of the Palace of Phaistos, in the south of Crete, no significant fortification has ever been found in connection with any building in the Minoan period. Also, if Minoan Crete was ever ruled by a royal dynasty, there is little evidence to be found of its existence. On the contrary, there is much more to suggest that Minoan civilization was radically different in composition from anything that followed it. Women appear to have had an important part to play in Minoan society. On murals and when depicted artistically on pottery or gold objects, Minoan women are the ones that stand out. They wear exotic clothes and are invariably shown being 'attended' by men, all of whom wear little or nothing in the way of adornment and who are invariably depicted doing homage to their female counterparts.

Does this indicate a totally matriarchal society? It is difficult to be certain, but the evidence does suggest that Minoan religion at least was dedicated primarily to an overall female deity, of the sort that also appears to have been worshipped across much of Western Europe from very early times. There is evidence of this, for example, in Malta, Cyprus, Spain, France and Britain. It also seems likely that Minoan civilization was 'consensual'. After all, as far as can be ascertained there was no standing army to keep the populace in check, no precautions taken to secure the wealth of the palaces in times of civil insurrection and in fact every evidence of a people who were generally prosperous and happy with their lot.

Perhaps this happy-go-lucky attitude died when the earthquakes, tsunamis and ash falls ravaged their homeland. The Minoans generally may have felt that the Great Goddess had abandoned them, and that it would be better to place themselves under the protection of more powerful, male deities. At this distance in time and with little concrete evidence, it is impossible to say. What is not in doubt is that Minoan society changed dramatically after around 1600 BC and it no longer reflected the uniqueness that had set it apart. The Minoan civilization had become strong and successful, but this had been achieved through trade; the Mycenaean way was quite different. True, the Mycenaeans forged themselves a sizeable empire, but it was achieved primarily through conquest. This was a very warlike culture, as indeed was the case for their Indo-European cousins the Hittites.

The Mycenaean culture was ruled by powerful kings, who doubtless fought their way to the top of their society. When they died, they were buried in sumptuous beehive tombs, surrounded by much of the wealth they had accumulated in life, and often wearing beaten-gold facemasks. This was a civilization that willingly took part in conquest, murder and slavery. It was the forerunner of the powerful and very militaristic city states that ultimately created what we now call classical Greece.

Mycenaean influence eventually spanned much of the Eastern Mediterranean, the Aegean and large parts of mainland Greece but the strength of the culture remained in the heartland of the Peloponnese, in heavily fortified cities such as Mycenae itself, together with Pylos, Orchomenos, and maybe also including Sparta and Glo in Boiotia. Doubtless much of what would eventually come down to us as classical Greece once fell under the sway of the all-powerful Mycenaeans. Their rule was brutal and absolute, with armed leaders predominating and much less evidence of a religious hierarchy than was clearly the case in Minoan Crete.

Prior to its connection with the Minoan civilization, the Mycenaean culture appears to have been illiterate and not particularly well organized – indeed there are some historians who would attest it wasn't really a civilization at all, until Minoan knowhow, seamanship, artistic and architectural skill and general organization were integrated into its running.

Just about everything related to the Mycenaean culture after the period between around 1600 and 1400 BC seems to have been heavily influenced by the Minoans. This might be another reason for wondering whether Crete was ever really conquered at all, or if what actually happened was a willing participation in the light of the Minoans' catastrophe. One gets the impression of a co-operation of such proportions that it is hard to imagine that it all came about as a result of Mycenaean pressure and violence. Even today, Cretans are not the sort of people that take kindly to being oppressed by outsiders. The adage 'better dead than a slave' still predominates on the island and one only has to look to the relatively recent past of the Second World War to see how willingly Cretans will fight and die in their efforts to defeat an occupying force.

Having looked at the situation carefully for many years, I cannot personally avoid feeling that what is today known as Mycenaean culture should really be termed Mycenaean/ Minoan culture. True, there is much that is clearly Indo-European about the civilization, including language, but in just about every other respect it has been heavily affected by what had gone before on the island of Crete and in its outposts.

Perhaps most significantly it seems to be the case that the Mycenaeans practised little in the way of overseas commerce until after their annexing of the Minoan culture. This is perhaps understandable: the pre-Greek Mycenaeans were the 'new kids on the block', whereas the Minoans had already been around and trading for many centuries. Like all other aspects of society, the Minoan navy, which had formerly been generally peaceful, became much more aggressive and warlike, though commerce continued on a significant scale.

The Minoans seem always to have been very efficient, especially in the way they produced food, clothing, metalwork and fancy goods for home consumption and especially for export. The level of organization at locations such as Knossos is obvious, with large magazines for the storage of every type of produce, stored there prior to cataloguing and dispatching to the ports. This was a skill that the Minoan civil servants and scribes took straight to the Mycenaean heartland. Linear B tablets from Mycenae and Pylos carry all manner of details regarding produce, but also detail the number of people employed at any particular palace site and indentify what they are doing.

The Mycenaean palaces may have had a similar function to those in Crete but with specific differences. Knossos was still running efficiently under Mycenaean rule, but by around 1400 BC it was definitely accountable not only to a king, but also to a high-ranking official who ran the military and to a succession of governors of various types. A certain amount of the free enterprise that appears to have flourished in purely Minoan times seems to have been retained. For example, a man could work predominantly for one of the palaces but there was little to prevent him from also managing his own enterprises if he wished.

Chief amongst the goods created by the Mycenaeans and used for export were fabrics of one sort or another. Again this is clearly a legacy of Minoan culture. Various types of cloth, both domestic and luxury, were produced, with wool being the most frequently used material, followed by flax. Huge herds of sheep were kept by the palaces, and presumably by ordinary people too. Those not employed by the palaces could belong to any one of a number of different trades or crafts. They were expected to pay taxes to the ruling elite and on a level below the ordinary citizens were both male and female slaves, the majority of which appear to have been employed in and around the palaces.

In addition to cloth, Minoan knowhow also conspired to make Mycenae a producer and an exporter of pottery, examples of which have been found a very long way from Greece. Though serviceable, and even on occasions beautiful, Mycenaean pottery did not have the flair or the technical wizardry of the earlier Minoan examples, when some vessels had walls as thin as eggshells. Nevertheless, decorated Mycenaean pottery demonstrates a strong Minoan influence, clearly heavily affected by Minoan tastes in art. What is more, examples of Mycenaean pottery have been found as far west as the British Isles.

Gradually, after the co-operation between Crete and the Mycenaeans began, there was a definite change in architecture in cities such as Mycenae and Pylos. In Mycenae especially, the masons began moving stone around on a grand scale. Western Europe had enjoyed a very long history of stone working and when it appears in Mycenae it is almost certainly a legacy of the knowhow of the pre-Indo-Europeans, who had erected huge stone structures as far east as Turkey, extending right across Europe to Britain. Thus we find in Mycenae a suffusion of cultural influence. Whilst the buildings and fortifications are most unlike anything seen formerly in Europe, the scale of the individual stones used is straight out of the European Neolithic. The walls of Mycenae are often referred to as 'Cyclopean', named after the one-eyed giants of Greek myth, who were said at later times to have been the only creatures with sufficient strength to quarry and lift such massive stones.

The cultural ancestors of the Mycenaeans had been pastoral nomads and seasonal hunters, with no experience in quarrying massive rocks, so it is surely certain that this skill was local and most probably Minoan.

From a religious point of view the Indo-Europeans had brought many of their old gods with them as they migrated west. This seems to have been one of the most significant departures as these people from the Central Asian Steppes eventually found their way into just about every nook and cranny of Europe.

Much of Europe, including Minoan Crete, had been responsive to an Earth-based religious adherence, in which a central, all-powerful goddess predominated. Just about all statuary found across the area, extending right back many thousands of years, depicted female forms. These are often extremely voluptuous depictions of the female form, with much-accentuated breasts and reproductive organs. These female representations are so common in the archaeological record of truly ancient Western Europe that there can surely be little doubt that they represent a significant religious imperative. From the same period, statuary depicting the male human form is almost totally absent. Gods may well have existed alongside the all-powerful Great Goddess of the Earth but if so they were not so commonly depicted in art.

It might be a controversial suggestion but it seems likely that the nature of the life led in varying locations probably had a great deal to do with the religious affiliations that ultimately developed. Although it can only be a general observation, indications are that life in Western Europe prior to the Indo-European migrations was generally fairly peaceful. If we take the British Isles as an example, farming had been present since at least 4000 BC and some recent agencies suggest that it probably extended significantly further back than this.

During the late Stone Age and early Bronze Age crops were grown in suitable areas, whilst livestock was kept in significant numbers, with sheep and cattle being the predominant species. Communities were small and the overall population not especially large. With what seems to have been a fairly quiet and generally pleasant climate predominating, everything people needed was supplied by the land. A low population density surely meant that battles over land acquisition were not common. At the same time, it is quite clear from some of the monumental structures that were created during the Megalithic period that cultural co-operation was not only evident, but extremely advanced. Some of the larger structures, particularly sites such as the Avebury rings in Wiltshire and even the giant henges in the north of England, would have required a large number of participants in their planning and construction. We also have to bear in mind the continuity of purpose and design that is evident from the very north of Scotland, right down into France. At every level there is a feeling of consensus and co-operation – a commonality of aspiration and purpose that indicates a cohesive culture, where even far-flung groups had much in common with their counterparts hundreds of miles away.

It is highly unlikely that massive sites such as the Yorkshire henges were only intended for the use of locals and we can undoubtedly see in them 'centres of pilgrimage' as well as places of trade and commerce. Huge later undertakings such as Stonehenge and Avebury may have brought like-minded individuals, sharing common lifestyles and beliefs, from far away to celebrate at specifically important parts of the year.

If we contrast this with what is known of the British Isles by the time the Indo-Europeans had arrived, we find a very different sort of picture emerging. The old Megalithic sites had fallen into disuse and more observable tribal divisions had developed. Signs of conflict had become much more obvious, whilst individual warriors – undoubtedly tribal leaders – began to be buried in their own separate graves, often surrounded by their possessions and weapons.

All of this is not too different from what was taking place far away, at the far end of the Mediterranean and in the Aegean. Weaponry was almost totally absent in either Minoan art or burials. Indeed, Minoan art was an almost total celebration of life, whereas with the dawn of Mycenaean influence and rule, a martial outlook on life – the glorification of war and weapons – becomes the norm. Faced with such similarities across vast distances, it would be hard not to look for the common factor between the Mediterranean region and Britain, which was of course the arrival of the Indo-European races after around 2000 BC.

It might be worth looking at the factors that had brought these people into Europe in the first place. Large-scale displacements of populations in ancient times were always a response to something that was happening locally. By common consensus the pre-Indo-Europeans had been both pastoralists and opportunist hunters. Any given area can only support a finite number of human beings and the conclusion must be that either a significant increase in population, or else changing climatic conditions forced these people on the move. It was inevitable that they would meet other human communities in the areas to which they migrated; if they wanted to secure new territory of their own, confrontation was sure to be the result. Such was their ultimate success that they eventually occupied just about all of Central and Western Europe. It is entirely logical to assume they were more aggressive than the indigenous populations they met.

Nevertheless, the destruction of already settled communities can never have been total. DNA testing of individuals in Britain has shown that some people's ancestry can be traced back many thousands of years to more or less the same location. A certain willingness to integrate is also demonstrated by the Mycenaean and Minoan association. If an indigenous population had something the newcomers needed or thought was useful, co-operation and interbreeding could and usually would be the result.

In terms of religious beliefs, it seems likely that the newcomers brought with them their own variety of aggressive 'storm god', which would be understandable in the case of a people who had inhabited the wild and open Steppes of Central Asia. It is interesting to see how well the Minoans managed to superimpose their own beliefs onto those of the more warlike Mycenaeans. Almost all artistic representations of deities appearing in Mycenae and its territories are female in gender. The only real difference between goddess representations from Crete and those of the Mycenaean period are that in Mycenaean art the goddess herself was often depicted with weaponry, which was never the case in original Minoan representations.

There are so few examples of male deities to be found in Mycenaean art that it was once thought that the whole of Mycenaean religion had come from the Minoans. However, once Linear B script had been deciphered and inscriptions read, it became obvious that the Mycenaeans also had a pantheon of their own powerful gods. These were the forerunners of gods that would also be important to Ancient Greece, long after the Mycenaean period. A figure very much like Zeus is evident, no doubt originally a Central Asian storm god – though some doubt is cast upon this suggestion because, even the later Ancient Greeks agreed that Zeus was originally a Minoan deity.

The Mycenaeans had also brought their own female deities from further east. They often created statues or frescos depicting sphinx-like creatures, though always with female human faces.

Little is truly understood of the end of the Mycenaean civilization and empire. Its demise spans the period when the Bronze Age was giving way to that of the Iron Age. Around the 12th century BC the citadel of Mycenae itself was acquiring even greater defences than it had once possessed, which could indicate that there was a threat of invasion. At about this time an even more warlike people, the Dorians, were starting to spread down into Greece, whilst what are known as the 'sea peoples', were attacking many states in the region from an unknown location in the Mediterranean. Neither seems to explain the decline of the Mycenaean world entirely and it is often suggested these days that the empire collapsed as a result of internal pressures: possibly uprisings amongst the lower classes of society, or struggles for power at the apex of the pyramid of state.

What is known is that the period around 1100 BC was one of turmoil across the Eastern Mediterranean and beyond. It was at this time that parts of the great Hittite Empire were destroyed and several major cities, such as Troy, appear to have been overrun and sacked. Distinctive aspects of Mycenaean culture disappear from the archaeological record and no trace is found after this time of the Linear B inscriptions that had been so common during the Mycenaean period.

It has been suggested that environmental factors may have been involved: for example, a succession of extremely wet or very dry years that led to a collapse in food output, with civil unrest being the result. Such a situation could have seriously weakened the ability of the Mycenaean and the Hittite empires to defend themselves, both from the newcomers streaming down from the north and from the constant attacks coming from the sea. Whatever the cause, the whole region entered what, until recently, was called the 'Greek Dark Ages'. It used to be supposed that this definable period lasted from the fall of the Mycenaean Empire, until around some time in the 9th century BC, when the Greek city states, which ultimately formed what we refer to as Ancient Greece, began to appear.

It is fascinating to conjecture that part of the tragedy that struck the area might have been due to an inability on the part of Mycenaean culture to keep up with the times. Iron work from Greece doesn't really appear until after the Mycenaean collapse, though it is evident in other areas from a much earlier date. In terms of defence, bronze is seriously inferior to iron when it comes to edged weapons and to the general strength of blades. Perhaps the influence of the Minoan spirit of innovation and inventiveness that had been present at the pinnacle of Mycenaean domination had been watered down with the passing of generations. So, when it was attacked by invaders who possessed iron weapons, the Mycenaean army could not respond.

It should not be inferred that life in the region ceased during the so-called Dark Ages. There is strong archaeological evidence that some areas continued to prosper, though most did not. Finds of pottery from the period tend to show local styles developing and there is generally less trade evident. Food production may have slumped and population levels seem to have fallen markedly.

All the same, the bright flame that had once been an independent Minoan civilization, which had burned less fiercely but steadily during the Mycenaean period, was certainly not extinguished during the Dark Age. On the contrary, the legacy of the Minoans was still quite perceptible when the city states developed and the glory that was Ancient Greece became a reality.

## Chapter 9

# 'Not so' Ancient Greece

Historians are fond of giving names to specific eras of the past. For example, they write glibly about the 'Bronze Age', when in fact the majority of people, for most tasks, still managed well enough with tools of knapped flint and obsidian. As another example, we talk about the Western European Renaissance, as if every individual would have been affected by an avalanche of new art forms, scientific realizations and stunning architecture, when in reality most people would have had no idea that anything different was taking place.

Similarly, the ordinary, average person living in what today is the country of Greece after the end of Mycenaean domination would have had little or no idea that he or she was living through a 'dark age'. Ordinary life doubtlessly went on as it always had. Farmers tilled the soil, picked the olives, herded the sheep and sold surplus produce at a local market. Artisans would have built small houses or slightly grander temples, potters would have turned out serviceable if not exactly elegant vessels for use in the kitchen and fishermen would have anxiously scanned the skies for signs of storms.

When it comes to assessing what was taking place in any given period of the past when there is no written evidence on which to rely, archaeologists only have the remnants of people's lives to go on. Whilst civilization continued on its course between the rivers Tigris and Euphrates and along the Nile in Egypt, a semi-transparent curtain was drawn across the Aegean for several centuries between the fall of Mycenae and around 750 BC. It is known from the archaeological records and from documents found in contemporary civilizations that during this dark age Greece experienced a great deal of Oriental influence from the Hittites, the Assyrians, the Egyptians and those great seafarers, the Phoenicians. Trade was still taking place and there doesn't seem to be any indication of an attempt by any of the existing civilizations in and around the region to take possession of Greece as a whole, so maybe the area was still quite good at defending itself.

It was around 750 BC that a new period, known as the archaic period of Ancient Greece began to dawn. In truth, little probably changed in the region from what had gone before, except for the fact that some of the developing city states began to communicate once more in the written word. The new alphabet owed nothing to the old Linear A or Linear B but was influenced by the growing connections with peoples to the east. From this period people were writing once more in Greek – both directly, and via later translations of long-lost documents, they began talking to us once more. In reality the Phoenician-derived Greek alphabet had been used for purely practical purposes from as far back as the 9th century BC, but it was closer to 450 BC when a writer named Herodotus, doubtless someone from a settled background and with time on his hands, began delving back a century or so before his own period and made himself into the so-called 'father of history'.

Chief amongst the developing city states of Greece was Athens, which is now the capital city of modern Greece. It was in Athens that culture and learning gradually became the norm. In any age, a developing interest in cataloguing the past and in formulating intellectual notions has to go hand in hand with stability and leisure. The average Iron Age farmer anywhere in Europe would have been fully occupied with all the chores that made life sustainable, but Athens was becoming organized enough to be able to support a hierarchy, which, thanks to slavery and a high degree of efficiency, made it possible for a small proportion of individuals to spend a large percentage of their time thinking, discussing and writing.

Thanks to them, we have a window on the period and can learn of the political, economic, religious and philosophical views of Athens, together with those of its companion city states. Whilst city states such as Sparta were developing their own unique forms of government, often as a result of the developing merchant classes rising up against their former aristocratic rulers, Athens, after its own troubles, managed to settle for a system in which a form of democracy developed, albeit one still run by a relatively small elite. As a result, Athens was able to defend itself from outside influence and entered its 'golden age'. It gained colonies in other areas and thrived on its trade, to the extent that the population rose markedly and the level of wealth throughout the city increased significantly. It was this wealth and relative stability that funded the rise of education. Institutes and libraries were created; like-minded individuals met to talk and debate, whilst their slaves at home took care of the practical necessities of life. Athens and its

127

companion city states became the epicentre of learning and as the archaic period gave way to the classical period, it created a written record upon which it is still considered that Western civilization was built.

The Greeks had always been a seafaring nation. The plethora of islands south of the mainland offered not only trading links but also a method of traversing large distances without ever being out of sight of land. Excursions through the Mediterranean along the southern coast of Europe remained possible, whilst the shores of the Levant also offered opportunities for trade, leading ultimately down to the Nile delta and the phenomenon that was Egypt.

The somewhat avaricious Athenians collected perfumes from Lebanon, gold from the Black Sea and rare minerals and amber, which had come overland from the Baltic, from Italy; they brought figs and dates from North Africa and also traded with the Egyptians. But beyond the luxuries that made life easier and more pleasant for the rich classes in Athens, the greatest prize brought back to Greece was knowledge.

There were probably many Greek writers at the dawn of the classical period of Greece who endeavoured to catalogue not only their own period but who also sought to understood something of history, and who collected accounts of contemporary civilizations and their achievements. Alas, many of these really early historians and commentators exist only as names, since what they produced has long since disappeared from the historical record. The earliest of these commentators whose work does survive was not an Athenian. His name was Herodotus and, although he was a Greek, he lived in Halicarnassus, in what today is Turkey. Herodotus (c484–426 BC) is often called the 'father of history', though he certainly did not approach his subject in the same way a modern historian would. His observations, contained in his only surviving book, entitled *The Histories*, were put together from existing works, supplemented by the author's personal observations and as a result of his own travels and investigations. The results of his efforts may not be absolutely accurate, but he did at least do his best to make his work ordered and sequential. In the absence of the work of other writers from the period, Herodotus provides a compelling picture of the ancient world and of the place Greece occupied within it.

The works of early Greek writers other than Herodotus are also intriguing and offer us insights not only into the way the archaic and classical Greeks viewed themselves and the world beyond their own shores, but also into the opinions they had of their own origins and their views on mythology and religion.

From Hesiod, an oral poet from between around 750 and 650 BC, we have an epic work known as the *Theogony*, an account of the Greek gods in chronological order, as well as a truly fascinating long poem created for his nephew which is entitled *Works and Days*. Comprising a truly compelling compendium of advice regarding how to live a successful, moral and happy life, as well as containing invaluable tips on farming, sailing, astronomy and a host of other subjects, *Works and Days* may be the best true glimpse into Iron Age life that we possess.

Another voice from the period, that of Homer (c850 BC), is famous for two amazing works that comprise a confusing mixture of myth and fact. These were the *Iliad*, which is an account of the Trojan wars, and the *Odyssey*, which is an adventure story about the epic quest of a mythical or semi-mythical hero named Odysseus. The *Iliad* and the *Odyssey* are the first and second oldest surviving works of Western literature.

These 'fathers' of Greek literature were known to and revered by thinkers and writers of the classical age. They lived centuries before Herodotus but he referred to them, indicating that more ancient works were available at the start of the classical era. It is a great pity that we cannot also read many of the other works used by Herodotus, copies of many of which were lost in catastrophes such as the destruction of the library of Alexandria and during numerous wars.

The Greek thinker and writer whose work I want to look at in the greatest detail was Plato. Plato was almost a contemporary of Herodotus. He lived in Athens between around 427 and 348 BC. Plato was born into an extremely wealthy and influential Athenian family and undoubtedly had the best possible start in life, especially in terms of education. By all accounts he was a quick learner and an avid student and eventually chose to study with the philosopher Socrates. In terms of much of Plato's writing we cannot be sure whether we are hearing Plato's own voice or that of his mentor Socrates. This is because Plato wrote a series of dialogues, which are intended as conversations, mostly between Socrates and other real or fictitious characters. Actually quoting Socrates, or using him as a useful device, Plato discussed all aspects of life from a philosophical viewpoint. Because of these extensive writings he is often referred to as the 'father of philosophy' and holds a unique place in Western thought.

The two works by Plato on which I want to particularly focus are two of his dialogues. They are known as *Timaeus* and *Critias*. *Critias* in particular mentions what most historians have considered since to be a purely mythical civilization, which Plato suggested occupied a large island in the Atlantic Ocean. This island he calls Atlantis. The characters in the dialogue suggest that there was a time when Atlantis and its people represented the greatest civilization in the world. Plato suggests that knowledge of Atlantis came to Greece via a supposed Athenian intellectual hero named Solon. Solon travelled to Egypt (around the 6th century BC) and there conversed with learned priests. It was these Egyptian priests who related the story of Atlantis, knowledge of which had supposedly been lost to the Greeks themselves.

According to the dialogue, Atlantis had existed until nine thousand years before Solon's visit to Egypt. Descriptions of the size of Atlantis show it to have been extensive, with a central palace and city on a wide plain, surrounded by mountains. The central part of the island could be approached by ships, which could berth in the metropolis, thanks to a series of circular canals which had been created for the purpose.

Plato reported that nine thousand years previously, Atlantis was waging war against peoples living in the Mediterranean region. The Atlantians had captured much of North Africa and also extensive parts of Europe, but were defeated in battle by the Athenians, who heroically liberated the captured parts of Europe and Africa.

Sometime after this event (we are not told how long) a series of terrible earthquakes and incredible floods not only swallowed the entire army of Atlantis, it also ultimately destroyed the island itself, causing it to sink into the sea, leaving behind it only shoals of mud and debris to mark where it had once been.

In the dialogue Atlantis is used as a suitable metaphor, in order to illustrate the point that is being discussed at the time. The account is unique because Atlantis does not figure in the work of Herodotus or any of the other Greek historians.

Neither is it mentioned in any known Egyptian account of history that has survived. Since Solon, the Athenian who was supposed to have received the information about Atlantis from Egypt, is himself almost entirely a mythical character it might be assumed that Plato fabricated the whole Atlantis myth simply to fund the conversation taking place in this particular dialogue.

In reality there are several reasons why the story of Atlantis as told by Plato cannot be historical fact. Chief amongst these is the fact that the story relates that Atlantis was at war with Athens, a full nine thousand years prior to Plato's own era. The archaeological record demonstrates that the region around Athens at this remote period was inhabited by hunter–gatherers – no civilization worth the name existed in Athens or anywhere else in the region at such an early date and so no cohesive force capable of taking on the supposed might of Atlantis could have been present.

As far as the description of Atlantis itself is concerned, according to geologists there never could have been a sizeable land mass in the mid-Atlantic region – the topography of the seabed simply doesn't allow for it. The Atlantic is an extremely deep ocean, which, unlike parts of the Pacific, has never created the sort of volcanic islands that fringe the Pacific Rim. It is true that sea levels were significantly lower at this time and more of the fringes of Western Europe would have been exposed and likely inhabited. This probably included what are now shallow areas of the North Sea between the British Isles and Continental Europe, but even if there was any trace of a major civilization in or around Britain at this early date – which there is not – the British Isles do not fit the geographical position indicated by Plato. Britain is well north of the Pillars of Hercules and may even have been still joined to mainland Europe nine thousand years ago.

Does this mean that we must dismiss the stories of Atlantis out of hand? This is certainly what most historians have done for at least a couple of centuries. There have been and still are diehard individuals who retain a belief in Atlantis, more or less as Plato described it, but these people do not come from the mainstream of historical academia. When defending their point of view such renegades invariably cite the case of Troy, which orthodox historians also considered to be nothing more than a myth, before Heinrich Schliemann found the city in the late 19th century. And in a way they have a point.

In order to judge the validity and accuracy of the story of Atlantis we have to look at the circumstances that prevailed prior to the rise of Athens and the life of Plato. The region had gone through a virtual dark age for several centuries. As I have suggested, it wasn't so much a dark age for the people who lived there as it is for us. Our failure to see back through the mists of time is mostly because with the fall of Mycenae writing disappeared from the region for a considerable period. People living in the area were therefore thrown back onto the oral traditions that have been the resource of human beings since the dawn of our awareness.

As with the famous children's game of 'Chinese Whispers', even stories that have a very real origin become distorted in the telling and the retelling. This was especially true in the case of the Greek region, where history could never be entirely divorced from religious mythology. We see this especially well illustrated in Hesiod's *Theogony*, which was written at the crucial period when oral traditions were once more giving way to the written word. In terms of genuine accounts of history,

133

related via literature, Plato and his contemporaries were looking back into a void and had only the stories they learned at their parent's knees and the religious cant of priests upon which to rely.

However, if experience has taught me one thing during the last four decades or more it is to never totally dismiss any story from the remote past without looking at it deeply. A very good example relates to Stonehenge, the structure in southern England that is famous the world over. In a very early British manuscript by a man named Geoffrey of Monmouth, which is entitled *The History of the Kings of Britain* and was written around 1136, Geoffrey relates that the stones comprising the circles at Stonehenge were brought to the site by the magician Merlin, from an already existent stone circle, far away to the west in Ireland. These days we would laugh at such an assertion. Merlin, who is a mythical character, is alleged to have lived around the 5th century AD, whereas we now know that the very latest phase of Stonehenge was complete by around 1700 BC.

The largest and most famous stones on the site are known as 'sarsens' and they were sourced in the area around Stonehenge, where similar boulders still exist. It is obvious then that what are known as the 'hanging stones', with their uprights and lintels, never had any association with Ireland.

Until comparatively recently it was accepted that every word of Geoffrey of Monmouth's account was based entirely on myth, but in the realms of ancient story cycles we should 'never say never'. The smaller horseshoe of stones that stands within the sarsens at Stonehenge are stones that are known as bluestones. More properly known as 'Preseli spotted dolerite', these stones cannot be found occurring naturally anywhere near Salisbury Plain, where Stonehenge is located. On the contrary, many of the bluestones are absolutely specific in origin, having come from the Preseli hills of Wales, over 250 miles to the west of Stonehenge.

Faced with this anomaly, for a while geologists tried to suggest that these stones had been brought to the Salisbury Plain by the action of glaciers, many thousands of years ago, but it has now been shown that this could not be the case, since no glaciation from South Wales to this area of southern England could have taken place without significant evidence being present, apart from the presence of the Bluestones. As a result there is only one conclusion that can be drawn: the bluestones at Stonehenge were deliberately brought, across mountain and bog, via rivers and coastal navigation to Stonehenge from South Wales. It is even possible that the bluestones did in fact already form all or part of an earlier stone circle in the Preseli hills, which was dismantled and transported east. Once at Stonehenge, the bluestones were redressed and erected on site.

Wales is not Ireland, but the Preseli hills do represent a place far to the west of Stonehenge, which of course is also the direction of Ireland. It becomes obvious therefore that the story told by Geoffrey of Monmouth was a garbled and misunderstood version of something that actually took place, over three thousand years before he put quill to parchment. This example alone proves how dangerous it is to ignore folk tales and legends, many of which can be found to have some basis in fact.

The period of time between the disaster that was Santorini and the life of Plato was nowhere near as long as that between the transportation of the Preseli bluestones and the life of Geoffrey of Monmouth. However, it was certainly long enough for any really important story, passed on for many generations via oral traditions, to have been garbled almost beyond recognition. Nevertheless, if we take the story of Atlantis to pieces, we can still see an essential truth beneath the centuries of embellishment and confusion.

In my estimation, what we are looking at here is not one story, but probably several, which have become enmeshed and intermingled. I have personally written several books dealing specifically with the Neolithic cultures of Western Europe and especially those of my own native Great Britain. Together with colleagues I have amply demonstrated that the knowledge possessed by the culture that created so many henges, standing stone circles and stone avenues across two thousand years was extensive. There is good evidence that these people were culturally related to, and kept good contact with, individuals in what is now France and also much further afield. The book *Before the Pyramids* that I wrote with Christopher Knight offers evidence that even the powerful priests in far-off Egypt were familiar with their counterparts in Britain and consulted them prior to the building of Egypt's most famous pyramids.

In other words, it was common knowledge, as much as four thousand years ago that there was a culture comprised of highly intelligent and mathematically adept people, just beyond the setting Sun, in the Atlantic ocean and on the Western fringes of Europe. I think race memories of these people, inflated and embroidered by constant retelling, form part of the stories of Atlantis. As we have seen, the Neolithic people of the British Isles were traders and seafarers, who were in possession of tin, a vital and very rare ingredient as the Bronze Age developed and progressed. High-ranking representatives of the culture would have found their way into the Mediterranean, where they would have been considered exotic, mystical and probably even powerful.

So far so good; we now have the origins of the land beyond the Pillars of Hercules, but what about the rest of the Atlantis story? What of the aggression between it and Athens and the part of the story that shows Atlantis disappearing in a single day as a result of a natural catastrophe?

At the time of the Santorini eruption, there was not a culture anywhere in the Mediterranean area that could compete in terms of technology, seamanship or cultural advancement with the Minoans. Representatives of Minoan culture were welcome and could hold their heads high in the court of the pharaohs in Egypt and doubtless also visited Sumer. At a time when life on the Greek mainland was still in a developmental stage, with small villages and loosely allied communities living a fairly hand-to-mouth existence, Minoans were building vast palaces with a thousand or more rooms. They had developed earthquake-resistant architecture, enjoyed deliberately planned water supply and drainage systems, which included flushing toilets.

It stands to reason that the amount of trade being carried on to and from Minoan Crete and its many outposts would have attracted avaricious eyes in the region. Minoan cargo ships would have been well worth hijacking, either on their outward or return journeys. It is for this reason that historians have always considered that the Minoans must have been in possession of formidable warships, which would have sailed in convoy with the merchant ships and which doubtless also patrolled the waters of the Eastern Mediterranean and the Aegean. Piratical raiders from the Greek islands or the mainland would undoubtedly have met with a swift and violent response. It was worthwhile for the Minoans to spend a fair proportion of their wealth on such measures, since the whole civilization rose or fell on the strength of its trade. It would therefore be surprising if Cretan sailors had not gained the reputation for being ruthless and powerful. In these facts we find the basis of the part of the story of Atlantis that shows the supposed culture at odds with at least some peoples from around the Mediterranean and maybe even beyond.

Finally we come to the demise of Atlantis – those horrendous earthquakes, born of the wrath of the god Poseidon, which brought an amazing civilization to a sudden and catastrophic end.

When the volcano on Santorini blew itself to pieces, most likely in 1628 BC, the implications were terrible, not only for the Minoan civilization, but for the whole surrounding area and even in some ways globally. Santorini itself is closer to Greece than is Crete. It most probably had its own direct trading links into the Aegean. Its powerful ships would be a regular sight and its colourful, intelligent people would have walked the shores of less well-ordered and far more primitive cultures. Like Atlantis, Santorini did, effectively, disappear within a day. Those on the mainland and in the Aegean could have been forgiven for believing that the catastrophe was due to earthquakes, because they themselves would have felt the resulting tremors caused by the eruption, as well as perhaps suffering from the resulting tsunamis.

At the same time, regular contacts with Crete itself would have been severely interrupted by the disaster. Much of the Minoan cargo and military fleet would have been destroyed on the north coast of Crete or in many of the culture's outposts. It probably took a decade or more before the culture lifted itself from the ash and debris, by which time, for reasons we don't fully understand, it had fallen under the influence of the Mycenaeans. To all intents and purposes, from the point of view of someone living in the Greek islands or on the southern mainland, the Minoan culture disappeared in a single day.

The various components of the myth of Atlantis, all of which had at least one foot firmly planted in race memory and actual fact, doubtless came together during generations of tales told over evening fires in Greek village communities. The memories of those advanced and intelligent people from the far west had originated at a time long before anything was committed to the written word, whereas at the time of the Santorini episode, Minoan Linear A was the only written language in the region. Its scribes were killed, relocated to Mycenae or committed to a new language. The story may have been told in writing, but if so its account was either destroyed or lies waiting for some future archaeologist's trowel.

Once Mycenae fell, there was no written language in Greece for several centuries and by the time written Greek appeared, the story cycles had become confused and intermingled. This, I believe, is the way the story of the fabulous Atlantis came about. At its heart is the true story of one of the most complete and utter disasters ever faced by our species. Effectively, the story is correct because to all intents and purposes an entire civilization did come to an end on a single day. As a result, the whole balance of population and power shifted, not only in the Eastern Mediterranean and the Aegean, but eventually across the whole of Europe, as the remorseless Indo-European juggernaut rolled inexorably westwards. How the continent would have developed if the Minoan civilization had survived and perhaps grown even stronger, we can never know.

In terms of my own research the operative fact is that, because of the vacuum caused by the destruction of Santorini and the dislocation of the Minoan civilization, Greece as a whole began to the look to the east for its ultimate culture and learning. The form of mathematics and in particular geometry that was ultimately embraced by the thinkers and mathematicians of classical Greece was only partly influenced by that which had developed in Europe, prior to the Indo-European invasions. But the older, European model had not disappeared altogether and so what we are now left with is an uneasy synthesis of two different ways of looking at and measuring our world. Most of my career has been spent in teasing the two systems apart, in order to view them both as they once were. One fact has become abundantly clear: the priests – the wise men and women of Europe – prior to the change of emphasis and influence after around 1600 BC had the better system, aspects of which are to be found lurking in the depths of mathematics and geometry to this very day.

## Chapter 10

# The Legacy and the *Phaenomena*

Around 276 BC a Greek poet from Cilicia was awarded the great honour of being invited to attend and serve the court of King Antigonus II Gonatas of Macedonia. The poet's name was Aratus and he was already well known amongst his peers, having met and studied with some of the greatest philosophers, writers and fellow poets of his period.

It was whilst living and working in Macedonia that Aratus wrote the only poetical work created by him that has survived to the modern era. It is known that he wrote many others but sadly these have not survived the ravages of time. The poem that does survive is actually two poems which are usually put together, though they are different in content and were almost certainly not written at the same time or intended to be combined. The title of the work is the *Phaenomena* and the first part, which runs to 732 verses, is an attempt by Aratus to describe the night sky in detail, with all its stars, planets, angles, changes and specifics.

It is generally accepted that Aratus was not, himself, an astronomer. On the contrary, in his handling of the *Phaenomena* he was recreating, though in verse, the observations of an earlier Greek, Eudoxus, who predated Aratus by around a hundred years. Legend has it that during his own lifetime, Eudoxus had expressed a wish that his work on astronomy could be presented poetically, which was very much the fashion in Greece at the time; obviously having a high regard for Eudoxus, Aratus fulfilled the astronomer's wish.

It is not necessary to test my readers by reproducing the astronomical section of the *Phaenomena*, which to those who are not of an astronomical frame of mind might seem somewhat tedious, not to mention confusing. All the same the *Phaenomena* is significant to my research in ways that would not seem immediately apparent.

One of the criticisms of the poem is that it does not specifically represent a view of the sky from Greece itself, or from the exact period of either Eudoxus or indeed Aratus. Generally speaking the stars in our sky are referred to as being fixed. What this really means is that from night to night they keep the same patterns, relative to each other, and can therefore be used as a reliable backdrop to the independent movements of the Sun, the Moon and the planets. Up to a point this is true, but not over protracted periods of time. The Earth not only turns on its axis each day, and orbits the Sun – it also wobbles slightly on its axis, somewhat like a child's spinning top. This is a very long-term occurrence because one complete 'wobble' takes around 26,000 years. A consequence of this is that when seen from the Earth the stars do change their positions slightly. This happening is known as the 'precession of the equinoxes'.

## The Legacy and the Phaenomena

It is therefore possible for astronomers today to work out exactly what the heavens looked like for both Eudoxus and Aratus, which is different than the accounts given in the *Phaenomena*. It is generally accepted that Eudoxus had been incorrect in his observations and that Aratus, not being an astronomer himself, simply copied Eudoxus' observations – mistakes and all. This seems odd to say the least because in his own time Eudoxus was well thought of and it seems very unlikely that an acclaimed astronomer could make significant mistakes in observation without his contemporaries having pointed out the fact.

Some decades ago professors of astronomy Archie Roy and Michael Ovenden of Glasgow University, noticed the discrepancies in the *Phaenomena* and wondered if not only Aratus but also Eudoxus had been using material from a different period and also from a different location on the planet's surface. With no particular conclusion in mind, both professors set themselves the intellectual task of trying to work out where and when (if ever) the sky as described by Eudoxus, and ultimately Aratus, would have made sense.

The process was long and complicated, particularly since at that time computers were nowhere near as useful in terms of historical astronomy as they are today, but both Ovenden's and Roy's eventual conclusions were that the operative date for the sightings of the sky expressed in the *Phaenomena* must have been around 2000 BC and had been made from a latitude of around 36° north of the equator. These findings were not taken particularly seriously. It is quite possible that the reason for this was that hardly anyone understood what they were saying, or rather that those astronomers who did understand had little or no interest in the remote past.

143

Ovenden and Roy's cause was taken up much later by Professor S Zhitomirsky from the Institute of Mechanics at Moscow State University. In 1999 he produced a paper for the *Journal of the Eurasian Astronomical Society*, entitled 'Aratus "phaenomena": Dating and Proving its Primary Source'. Professor Zhitomirsky was meticulous in his methodology and deliberately used a different method to the ones employed by Ovenden or Roy. After exhaustive investigations he came to the conclusion that Ovenden and Roy were absolutely correct. There was nothing at all wrong with Aratus' description of the heavens, or the position of the constellations and their angles relative to the horizon and each other, except for the fact that Aratus was describing something that was nearly 1,500 years out of date and in a different geographical location from where he composed the poem.

The inference must be that Eudoxus had also been relying on truly ancient information when he created the non-poetical and original version of the *Phaenomena*, which Aratus had simply accepted and set to verse.

If we cast around the planet and also make reference to ancient history, there is only one place on the planet in which a major civilization flourished in 2000 BC and which was also around 36° north of the equator, and that was Minoan Crete. The other major civilizations of the period, those of Egypt and the Sumerians, were significantly further south. Zhitomirsky did not speculate as to the information having come from Crete, but to Ovenden and Roy it had been the only logical conclusion. The *Phaenomena* of Aratus, and ultimately of Eudoxus, described an extremely accurate picture of the daily and seasonally changing sky as seen from the northern shores of the island of Crete.

# The Legacy and the Phaenomena

Professor Zhitomirsky attempted to answer the thorny question of how Eudoxus may have come by this information and concluded that the work must have been culled from oral traditions since there appears to be no way that any written references could have survived the centuries of the Greek 'dark age' and spanned the period between Minoan Crete and classical Greece. This seems to be a very reasonable assumption, except for one very significant fact, to which the learned professor did not have access.

The part of the *Phaenomena* that deals specifically with astronomy, as put in verse by Aratus, contains exactly 732 verses. 'So what?' I hear you ask. In order to see what this might mean we have to cast our minds back to an earlier chapter, in which I mentioned that not only the Minoans, but peoples as far west in Europe as the British Isles, had used a form of geometry that assumed 366° to a circle. Alexander Thom had shown that structures built in the British Isles during the Neolithic period had been created using a standard unit of measure, the Megalithic yard. Later, Christopher Knight and I demonstrated that a larger unit of 366 Megalithic yards had been repeatedly employed, particularly in the building of the giant henges of the British Isles. However, the builders often doubled this unit, so that structures of 732 Megalithic yards are extremely common. In a real sense the number 732 was as important to these people as was 366.

Can we see Aratus' use of 732 verses for the *Phaenomena* as being strictly coincidental or are we looking at the retention of knowledge that relied on something far more specific than the caprices of merely routine oral traditions? In reality, to conclude that the material in the *Phaenomena* could be a simple case of information passed on casually by word of

145

mouth would be quite incredible. We are, after all, talking about almost 1,500 years and the transmission of fairly complicated facts and figures between two quite different cultures and languages.

Whether or not Aratus did choose 732 verses deliberately and was part of some enduring fraternity that continued to understand 366° geometry, it is obvious from the meticulous work of Ovenden, Roy and Zhitomirsky that as early as 2000 BC the Minoans had an excellent understanding of the sky and the many nightly and seasonal changes it underwent. They must have been aware of the angle of inclination of the Earth and almost certainly also knew about the complex procession of the equinoxes. Professor Zhitomirsky, no doubt cognizant of his position and career, was clearly careful in terms of suggesting the historical implications of his findings. On several occasions he did, however, mention these findings in connection with the possible knowledge of astronomer priests much further west in the British Isles. Bearing in mind the *Phaenomena* and the evidence supplied by three eminent astronomers, no serious observer could doubt that the Minoans and their contemporaries in the far west were competent astronomers and mathematicians and that a wealth of information possessed by them found its way across two millennia to the shores of mainland Greece.

I am truly grateful that this evidence exists because it shows conclusively that astronomy and geometry were not the preserves of classical Greece but predated it in a wholly European form by more than 1,500 years. As a result it became obvious that the classical Greeks were struggling under not one, but two forms of geometry. Since neither Eudoxus or Aratus admit to being party to anything other than the astronomical conventions of their day, it is surely likely that the European model formed part of some 'hidden' system, which existed alongside the 360° geometry that had come from the Sumerians during the long Greek dark age. This is borne out by the fact that the picture of the sky they both set out in their respective versions of the *Phaenomena* was well out of date in their own era and at the location where they lived and worked, a fact that must have been known to Eudoxus, even if not to Aratus.

At the time I first laid eyes on the Phaistos Disc, I had never heard of Aratus or the *Phaenomena*. My initial observations told me that the disc represented the number sequences necessary for the rectification calendar, as mentioned in a previous chapter. It was only later, and in conjunction with Alexander Thom's evidence concerning the Megalithic yard and J Walter Graham's research into the Minoan foot that I began to see shades of astronomy in the disc.

# What is Geometry and Where Did it Come From?

The word geometry literally means 'to measure the Earth', from the words 'geo' for Earth and 'metron' to measure. So although geometry these days is generally seen as quite distinct from our planet, and a means by which we can measure angles quickly and accurately, that is not how it began.

I puzzled for many years over the origins of the 360° circle. I could see that it had a correspondence with the year, as measured by ancient cultures such as the Sumerians, but what was more difficult to ascertain was whether circles had 360° to match the theoretical year, or if the civic year in the Sumerian civilization had been fixed at 360 days in order to better fit a proposed geometry.

It has to be admitted that when it comes to splitting circles, 360 is an ideal number. This is because it is divisible by so many other numbers, without having to resort to fractions or decimals, which would not have been easy for our ancient ancestors to deal with. The number 360 is divisible by 2, 3, 4, 5, 6, 8, 9 and 10, so it could hardly be a more useful number in this regard. For the Sumerians it was especially useful in terms of their system of numbers. In modern times we use a decimal system of counting, which relies on the number 10. The Sumerians also relied on 10, but in addition they were fixated on the number 6, so they counted in blocks of 6 x 10 = 60. Aspects of this system are still around and in fact we use them every day, both in geometry and in the measurement of time. In geometry, there are 60 minutes of arc to every degree and 60 seconds of arc in every minute of arc. Timewise we have 60 seconds to the minute and 60 minutes to each hour. What was specifically difficult for me to understand at first was why the same terminology, minutes and seconds, was used for both geometry and time when there appears to be no direct connection between the two. In other words, one minute of time is not the same thing as one minute of arc of the Earth turning on its axis. It actually takes the Earth around four minutes of time to turn on its axis by one whole degree of arc.

Eventually, in a flash of insight, the whole Sumerian way of dealing with time and geometry became clear to me and as far as I can tell I was the first person in several thousand years to rebuild this part of the Sumerian system of mathematics.

It is first necessary to realize that the Sumerians, like all civilizations, had gone through a process of evolution. In its earlier stages, Sumerian society had been committed to measuring time by way of the Moon. As seen from the Earth, the Moon takes just over 29.5 days to pass from its first slim crescent, through its phases to full Moon and then back again via the new Moon to that first observable crescent. This was the origin of the Sumerian month and indeed the word month derives from the word 'Moon'.

So, originally, to the Sumerians and indeed to most people in the Near and Middle East, it was the Moon that ticked off the 12 divisions of the year, with each month commencing at the first sight of the new Moon. In fact some cultures still rely on this method of judging the duration of months.

The problem comes when some wise individual within Sumerian society realized that there are more than 12 lunar cycles in an Earth year. In reality, 12 lunar cycles is equal to only 354.4 days – which eventually seemed inconvenient and unwieldy to the tidy-minded Sumerian priests and scribes.

When the situation is looked at closely it becomes obvious that quite early in Sumerian history someone took the decision to consider the lunar cycle to be not 29.53 days, but a round 30 days. It is upon this fact that the whole of geometry and modern-day time keeping is based. The only other factor we have to bear in mind before we reconstruct the Sumerian system is that there were originally only 12 hours in a day. The day was split into 24 hours later, long after the true genius of the Sumerian system had been forgotten.

To the Sumerian astronomers the Moon did not simply pass from new to full and back again – it also travelled once around the heavens during its phase cycle. In other words it completed a circle. If they split that circle of 30 days into 360, as they also split the year into 360 days, each 1/360th of the Moon's 30-day orbit would take 1/12th of an Earth day. This is where the hour originally came from. It is, theoretically, the time taken for the Moon to travel 1/360th part of its journey around the Earth.

It has to be stressed that none of this system is 'absolutely' true and it is certain that the Sumerian scribes knew that is wasn't. There are discrepancies at every stage but these could be compensated for when an extra month was added to the year each time it became necessary. What mattered was that this way of measuring the year, the month and the day, as well as the hours, minutes and even seconds of the day was uniform and logical, which the heavens were not.

Here we have the origins for both time keeping and geometry, which to the Sumerians were one and the same thing. To the scribes the sky was divided into 360 segments, as was the day and also the very Earth itself. It wasn't too much of a leap in logic to assume therefore that 'any' circle could be divided into 360 segments, and that each segment could be further divided into 60 minutes and each minute divided yet further into 60 seconds. It was a stroke of genius that eventually led to the efficient handling of mathematical problems associated with shapes and angles.

During the intervening period, with all the comings and goings of humanity – its rising and falling civilizations and its changes in civil and religious administrations – both the geometry and the method of time keeping first dreamed up by the Sumerians have been maintained. Unfortunately, it is clear that not everyone at every stage was conversant with the 'reasons' for the system. As a result, the day was eventually split into 24 hours instead of 12. When this happened, the correspondence between the original lunar geometry and the measurement of time was lost. To the Sumerians, time and distance on the Earth were intimately related, but by the start of the modern era the correspondence had been so mutilated that it was hardly recognizable.

# The 366° System

The essential difference between the Sumerian 360° system and the European 366° system lay in the fact that the Sumerian model was based on the movements of the Moon, whereas the European model relied on the apparent movements of the Sun. The European astronomers, in Minoan Crete and elsewhere (including those of the British Isles) adopted a year of 366 days, which they corrected by way of the secondary calendars mentioned earlier.

Each year the Earth travels once around the Sun, which from a naked-eye perspective looks as though it is travelling around the Earth. Meanwhile, each day the Earth turns one complete revolution on its own axis. To these early astronomers the day was simply a microcosm of the year. They reasoned that if the year could be split into 366 units, then so could the day. As with the Sumerian system, for convenience the year was split into 12 units – we can't really call them months because they were not fixed by way of the Moon. These units were of 30 and 31 days alternately. So for example, January would have 30 days, February would be 31 days in length, March would have 30 days and so on, but the true genius of the system lies in the fact that time and distance were measured in exactly the same way.

As far as the size of the polar Earth (circumference of the Earth via the poles, rather than round the equator) was concerned, one degree of time was exactly the same as one degree of distance. The truly amazing fact about the 366° system is that those who used it quite clearly had an incredible understanding of the true dimensions of the Earth. We know this is the case because the basic units of measurement, the Megalithic yard in the far west and the Minoan foot in Crete, were 'geodetic' units. This means they divide equally (and obviously intentionally) into the polar circumference of the Earth.

The Sumerian system, which in its own way was also extremely clever, was never geodetic in terms of its basic linear units, though it did win out over the Megalithic system in that it was far more useful for abstract geometry, simply because its 360° were so readily divisible by whole numbers.

## The Ravages of Time and Oral Cultures

If all of this is true, why is it that the whole world now relies on what is essentially Sumerian geometry and time keeping – albeit a version that has been tortured almost beyond belief? There are a number of reasons for this state of affairs.

First and foremost we have never found any sort of numerical notation from the period in the British Isles or France when the henges and stone circles of the Neolithic period were being built. It is unlikely that every single trace of a written language would have escaped the eagle eyes of archaeologists. It is true that the soils here in the far west of Europe, together with the wet climate, are not ideal for preserving organic material. So, if alphabetical components or numerical information had been written in some form of script on, say, tree bark, we could not expect this sort of material to survive well when buried.

All the same, my own early expeditions into archaeology, particularly in the city of York, taught me that under specific circumstances, all manner of organic material 'can' survive for many centuries. Leather and fabric from the Viking period have regularly been found in York, where the specific conditions had allowed them to be starved of oxygen and therefore preserved from decomposition. Similarly, organic material from remote antiquity has been discovered in bogs, for the same reasons.

Nevertheless, the conclusion must surely be that much of Western Europe never developed alphabetical or numerical writing during the period at which the pre-Indo-European cultures flourished. There are complex patterns carved into stone to be found in all manner of locations, which comprise simple indentations, spirals, swirls, lozenges and a host of other figures, but if they are intended to be communication we have not yet come anywhere near to understanding what they are trying to tell us.

We need not be too surprised about this. The basic rules of the 366° system are essentially quite simple. It is also a fact that extremely complex information can be passed on, generation to generation, by way of oral tradition and specific teaching. A continuing priesthood could have seen young individuals being schooled for many years in the history, traditions and mathematics of a culture. This would not have been a unique situation. Anthropologists have discovered very complex information carried across generations by word of mouth in locations all around the world.

The type of culture flourishing in pre-Indo-European Europe was very different to that which evolved in the Near and Middle East. There never seems to have been large conurbations or city states and although a great deal of cohesion between often far-flung peoples seems to have existed, there was never any need for complex lists of merchandise, food or land divisions – which was certainly the key to written language developing in the Sumerian world.

The only exception is Minoan Crete, which did develop writing. It is most likely that this happened because of the island's specific needs and requirements. It was geographically very different to other parts of Western Europe and the needs of its people were also different. If the Minoans wished to flourish and prosper, they had to rely almost totally on trade, to supply the raw materials their own island home lacked. Initially at least the Minoans may also have taken a leaf out of the book of their Egyptian neighbours. The first Minoan alphabet was hieroglyphic and bears a striking resemblance to that of the Egyptians, so there may be a connection.

Even in the case of the Minoans, there is every reason to believe that, in the main, their astronomical skill, with its obviously associated religious imperatives, relied on oral traditions. Both prior to the Santorini eruption and afterwards, the Minoans became great at keeping written lists – as were the Egyptians and the Sumerians, but, aside from the Phaistos Disc, there is no written evidence relating to astronomy or geometry. Why this is the case we may never know, and of course it is entirely possible that more evidence will be discovered at some, as yet undiscovered, Minoan site.

What we retain is the 'ghost' of an extremely clever, orally transmitted, system. It can only be fully resurrected from random pieces of evidence. We can find it in the length of the Minoan foot, and in the Megalithic yard. As a result it speaks to us in terms of the size of structures, both in Crete, across the Mediterranean islands and in the far west of Europe. It also comes to us through poems such as the *Phaenomena*, which has been quite clearly shown to relate directly to Crete at a time contemporary with the height of the Minoan civilization.

The situation reminds me of something I once read regarding the true horror of the atomic bomb that was dropped on the Japanese city of Hiroshima in 1945. When people began to investigate the ruins, shortly after the explosion, they were astounded to see the shadows of people, burned into masonry that was still standing. Such had been the power and the heat of the catastrophe that the bodies of the people concerned had been totally incinerated, but because their presence had shielded parts of the wall where they had been standing, a ghostly shadow remained. The presence of these truly unfortunate individuals cannot be doubted. They existed, and so did the magnificent Megalithic system, replete with both genius and simplicity.

It is even possible that there had always been a genuine taboo about committing the system to the written word and that it *did* survive that long-lost epoch amongst specific families or peoples. This certainly seems to be the case when we consider Aratus and his 732 verses of the *Phaenomena*, which is surely another shadow of the original system, somehow kept safe and sacred for upwards of 1,500 years. Was its working matrix lodged in the secret academies of classical Greece, or enshrined into the mystery religions that proliferated throughout the Greek world? Did it form part of the mystery school of Pythagoras? Clearly the classical Greeks learned much from it. The understanding of the heavens demonstrated by the *Phaenomena* was greater than anything ever achieved by the Sumerians, the Babylonians or the Egyptians, and yet its ancient pedigree proves it was not the work of the classical

Greeks either. To them it was a starting point to their own growing knowledge and might be said to be the foundation of all subsequent knowledge in astronomy.

The shadow of the 366° system also survives in other, even more surprising ways. When Christopher Knight and I looked closely at the Sumerian system it became obvious to us that all of the measuring systems they had used were also ultimately based on their 360-day year and 360° geometry. They had used a unit of linear measure known as the 'kush'. How they arrived at this unit, which is extremely close to 0.5 metre, is fully explained in our book *Civilization One*. The Sumerian units of weight and volume were derived from the kush. A cube with sides that measure 1/5th of a kush, when filled with water, leads to the Sumerian unit of weight known as the 'mana' and also the volume unit called the 'sila'.

Imagine our utter surprise when we discovered that a cube with sides measuring 1/10th of a Megalithic yard, when filled with water, leads exactly to a unit of volume identical to the modern imperial pint, whilst if the same cube is filled with barley or wheat seeds and the seeds are then weighed, the result is equal to one modern pound!

The statement that 'history is written by the victor' is invariably true. Science these days relies totally on the remnants of the Sumerian system of geometry and time measurement. Superimposed on this is the modern convention of considering the year to be 365 days in length, a discrepancy that is compensated for by the use of leap years. The 360° geometry system works extremely well – so well in fact that it has become a 'given'. In other words it doesn't occur to anyone that any different form of geometry could ever have existed. Despite the fact that the 366° system leads directly to units of measurement that were used all across the British Empire until the adoption of the metric system, and which are still used in the United States, and even though practically every Megalithic structure in Britain and France was based upon its companion linear measurements, as were those of Minoan Crete, not one single supposed expert has so much as looked at the situation.

This is unfortunate to say the least. Those who devised the 366° system were fully conversant with the polar circumference of the Earth. Even more astounding is the fact that the system also seems to have had a correspondence with the mass of our planet.[1] This was a system that measured time, distance, mass and volume, using the same numbers throughout and without ever requiring a number to be split. Perhaps it is the full scope of what we came to call the Megalithic system that frightens those whose job it is to look at ancient history. After all, it would take courage indeed to admit that at least six thousand years ago, apparently unsophisticated farmers, living in an age during which even metal had not been tamed, possessed and used an integrating measuring system that makes our present metric system look slightly cumbersome by comparison.

---

1   See Christopher Knight and Alan Butler, *Civilization One*, Watkins, 2011.

## Chapter 11

# Mind Versus Machine

At some stage in our lives, even if it is only during our child-hood, most of us dream of finding treasure. We are captivated by the gleam of gold and silver, to the extent that Schliemann's unearthing of Troy and Howard Carter's discovery of the tomb of Tutankhamen not only made headlines all over the world at the time but also promoted changes in art, fashion and popular literature. Perhaps the very best sort of treasure comes when the finder was actually looking for something completely different, as was the case in the Aegean at the very start of the 20th century.

In the year 1900, at almost exactly the same time that Arthur Evans was working on a difficult set of political strategies what would allow him access to the Knossos site in Crete, a group of sponge divers were busy combing the waters around the Greek island of Antikythera. During the autumn they came across something that was to make history: they discovered an ancient shipwreck, in shallow waters and in relatively good condition.

The ship was a treasure-trove and had undoubtedly been on its way to Rome, most likely to celebrate one of Julius

Caesar's triumphs, or alternatively its cargo was destined for auction amongst the rich citizens of Rome. The contents of the sunken ship were not what one might normally expect for cargo vessels of the period – for example grain, oil, wine, olives, etc. – but rather a wealth of treasures culled from the Greek world and beyond.

Included amongst the cargo were marble and bronze statues, beautiful articles in pottery and glass, coins of many different sorts and other objects that the Greek-loving Roman upper crust would have adored. The range of objects in the vessel, and in particular the coins, made it possible to date the wreck to a period between 80–50 BC. Some of the objects included in the cargo were very much older, indicating that they were already antiques when they were purchased or looted from Greece. The cargo as a whole is justifiably famous but there was one object brought up from the wreck that was not identified at the time, and which sat around in an Athens museum for two years before it was even looked at. It appeared to be a concretion, containing remnants of wood and metal, but it wasn't until 1902 that it was noticed that within the mass there were what appeared to be corroded toothed gear wheels.

Anything of the sort from such a remote period was clearly ludicrous, and it was assumed for a long time that whatever this mass of wood, metal and concretion was, it must have come to be on the site of the shipwreck from a very much later time than the wreck itself.

It wasn't in fact until 1951 that anyone's attention turned to the object again in any serious sense. It was at that time that an English-born mathematician and physicist by the name of Derek J de Solla Price became interested in the object. Having seen it in the museum and read earlier reports, de Solla Price determined to know more about what would eventually come to be called the 'Antikythera Mechanism'. It was impossible to establish anything really tangible regarding the object until as late as 1971 when de Solla Price, together with a Greek nuclear physicist named Charalampos Karakalos, was able to X-ray the many fragments, which by this time had mostly been pried free of the concretion. It soon became obvious that the various components had once contributed to a very sophisticated mechanical device, which, on account of carrying inscriptions in a form of Greek that was common at the period, was shown to be contemporary with the shipwreck.

Whatever the Antikythera Mechanism was, it positively shocked historians because it had been far more sophisticated than any device previously known to have originated in the classical Greek world – or indeed from anywhere else at such a remote period. It eventually became apparent that the device had been intended as some sort of astronomical device – this much was obvious from many of the inscriptions. The logical conclusion was that it must have been a planetarium or orrery of some sort, designed to track the positions of the Sun, Moon and possibly the planets, but in the early stages of research into the mechanism nobody could have even dreamed just how sophisticated it had been.

A succession of individuals created computer simulations or actual mechanical re-creations of the device. Thousands of hours of patient observation, thought and trials went into trying to replicate what the original mechanism might have looked like and attempting to understand what it was designed to do. It would be fair to suggest that even the existence of the Antikythera Mechanism was enough to force a rewriting of known capabilities of engineers in Ancient Greece.

Using the gear wheels that do remain, together with the Greek inscriptions, investigators have learned a great deal about the Antikythera Mechanism. It was originally housed in a wooden box, which carried both dials and inscriptions on the front and the back, with the back in particular given over to what some researchers have called the 'instruction manual'. Not much of this latter has survived but enough to know certain things about the mechanism's purpose.

The Antikythera Mechanism was essentially 'clockwork' in that the user turned a handle on the front of the device, which was connected to a toothed gear wheel. This meshed with other gear wheels, the size and number of teeth of which had been carefully calculated. No other device as sophisticated as this is 'known' to have existed until the invention of clocks in Europe 1,400 years later, and even then it would have taken another century or two for clockmakers to achieve the technological and mechanical prowess of whoever planned and made the Antikythera Mechanism. This is partly because most of the gear wheels of the mechanism are quite small, with teeth that are tiny. It would have been necessary to make these using extremely accurate marking devices and ultimately with files.

Engineers, clockmakers and modellers take extremely fine files, often known as needle files, for granted. Files themselves carry a rasp-like arrangement of sharp teeth, which bite into and remove the metal of the object being engineered. It would be difficult enough to create the fine teeth on the gear wheels of the mechanism, though these are made from bronze, metal that is fairly soft. However, it would be something else entirely to create the tiny files necessary to do the job. These would have to be made of iron, or more likely steel – allowing for the technology of the period in question, they would be extremely awkward to create. My own background in mechanical engineering tells me that the tools needed to make the Antikythera Mechanism would have been much more difficult to manufacture than the device itself. If only for this reason it is highly unlikely that the device found on the shipwreck was the only example of its kind.

The mechanism also implies 'evolution'. It would be impossible for anyone, without real skill, acquired across many years, to create such a clockwork masterpiece from scratch. It is most unlikely that such skills would have been invented and mastered in one lifetime. In the medieval period and beyond, the making of machines developed from earlier techniques acquired in the art of blacksmithing. It was a long and arduous process. Even the first European clocks tended to be large-scale devices, in which absolute precision was to be desired but rarely if ever achieved. By the time clocks were being created with gear wheels the size of those in the Antikythera Mechanism, several generations of learning, refining and fine-tool making had elapsed.

The inference is that the Antikythera Mechanism was produced by craftsmen or women who were undoubtedly following a tradition of such practices. The great thinkers of classical Greece might have designed such devices but unless they dedicated themselves to the necessary skills for years, they are unlikely to have made their own masterpieces. There is nothing remotely clumsy or primitive about the device and even the Greek inscriptions appear to have been incised into the bronze by a practiced hand, using sophisticated gravers. The true artisans involved might as likely have come from a background in art as one in engineering. Many mechanical devices which did exist at the time and which we know about because they were copied by the Romans – such as components for water mills and the like – were made of wood or were created with hammers and lots of human effort working at forges. These were a world away from the clockwork genius of the Antikythera Mechanism.

What remains self evident is that someone did indeed create the Antikythera Mechanism, since it was amongst the cargo of the sunken ship and is reliably dated to the same period. But if the secrets of its manufacture beggar belief, what it could do is far more surprising still.

Ideas differ as to the ultimate complexity and capabilities of the device but nobody doubts that it kept a fairly accurate measure of the passing of days, that it showed the position of the Sun and the Moon within the zodiac and that it likely originally also tracked the movements of the planets known to the Greeks. Further to this, the mechanism was also capable of predicting eclipses – which itself is a fiercely complicated business and relies on the knowledge of what are known as 'Saros cycles'. The mechanism also displayed the phases of the Moon, thanks to an ingenious mechanical method of a sort that was not known again for many centuries; it also predicted the years at which athletic games would occur, not only at Olympus but also in other areas of the Greek world. All of this and more was made possible in a compact space and with the turning of a single handle.

The various tasks of the device were achieved by way of gear trains, which are successions of different-sized gear wheels, each containing different numbers of teeth, which change the ratios of the gear trains, in turn passing information to dials on the front or rear of the device. If, as a mechanical engineer, I was tasked with creating a machine that could achieve all the functions of the Antikythera device, even allowing for an advanced knowledge of astronomy and the use of modern electronic calculators and computer aided design, it would take years for me to complete such a task. The successful completion of such a machine using only the accepted knowledge and technology of two thousand years ago is little short of breathtaking.

What makes the various tasks of the Antikythera Mechanism so difficult to achieve is the fact that it is a clockwork device, composed of toothed wheels. Such devices work very well – for example, the gearbox of your car almost certainly works in the same way – but although the solar system and its many cycles can be equated to a gearbox, it isn't really quite that simple.

Let us look again at the length of the year. Depending on what 'sort' of year one intends to track (because there are a number of different sorts of year) a simple gear wheel with teeth could never define the number. This is because the length of the year does not correspond to an even number of days. The sidereal year is equal to 365.2564 days and so would require a gear wheel with '365 and a bit' teeth, which of course is impossible. The Moon is just as unhelpful. The Moon's full journey around the Earth when viewed with respect to a fixed star is around 27.322 days, whereas its full range of phases, from new, through full and back to new again is around 29.53 days. To get even these three factors to work accurately by way of gear trains is almost impossible. Indeed, even with the Antikythera Mechanism it was necessary to compensate for the Earth year by adding an extra day every four years manually.

When we add in the fact that the device also dealt with other complicated factors, such as Saros cycles and various other types of year, it is a near miracle that it works at all, and only does so thanks to an array of additional bits of engineering 'magic' incorporated into the mechanism. Some of these are truly ingenious and they contribute to a device that was as accurate as anything created prior to the 17th century in Europe. However, it is important to remember what was said by Tony Freeth and Alexander Jones, the writers of 'The Cosmos in the Antikythera Mechanism', a paper reprinted in 2012:

> the Antikythera Mechanism was a machine designed to predict celestial phenomena according to the sophisticated astronomical theories current in its day, the sole witness to a lost history of brilliant engineering, a conception of pure genius, one of the great wonders of the ancient world – but it didn't really work very well![2]

Whilst I find this statement somewhat disingenuous, I cannot claim that it is untrue. Such is the complex nature of the tasks the Antikythera Mechanism was designed to undertake, it is hardly surprising that it 'nearly' achieves them all but fails to complete any of its various jobs truly accurately. It took another true genius, the Englishman John Harrison (1693–1776), most of his adult life to create a chronometer that was robust enough to endure life at sea and which still kept incredibly accurate time. This undoubted feat was as nothing compared to what the Antikythera Mechanism was expected to achieve. Harrison had the advantage of a rapidly developing technological infrastructure to back his efforts

---

2   Tony Freeth and Alexander Jones, 'The Cosmos in the Antikythera Mechanism', ISAW Papers, reprint 2012.

– replete with great advances in tool making and huge leaps forward in mathematics – and even then his chronometer did not keep 'absolutely' accurate time.

It is generally accepted that much of the knowledge used to create the Antikythera Mechanism was not home grown in Greece. Most experts agree that elements of its working matrix owe a great deal to the Babylonians, who themselves were legatees of the Sumerians in Mesopotamia. This is especially true in the case of eclipse prediction, which the Babylonians had mastered to a high degree. The creators of the Antikythera Mechanism also based their device on the year of 365.25 days, which had also most likely come from Babylon. As we have seen, this was wrong from the start, so inaccuracies were bound to creep into the system from the outset. These might not seem like much, but across time they add up, so that after several hundred complete turns of the mechanism's handle, it would be offering nothing more than a fairly rough approximation of any of its intended information. In this sense at least, and despite the breathtaking fact that it exists at all, the Antikythera Mechanism is much less accurate than the Phaistos Disc, which predates it by maybe two thousand years!

It is far from easy to deal with fractions of numbers via simple mechanical means, and in any case the ancients were not generally comfortable in dealing with fractions at all – they much preferred whole numbers. The Babylonians had found ways to split numbers, as had the Egyptians, but neither civilization was either very adept at doing so, or particularly accurate. Even in terms of the true length of the Earth year, experts would have us believe that it wasn't known exactly until extremely recently – so how could it ever have been possible for our distant forefathers to keep a truly accurate track of the solar system's cycles?

The Sumerians and their later counterparts the Babylonians had dealt with the problem of splitting numbers in a clever way – and one that remains with us today. Their method was to turn big things into known numbers of smaller things. By so doing they continually kept the problem of fractions or decimals at a distance. Take, for example, 1.5 days. The Sumerians or Babylonians would have called this time period 1 day and 6 hours (because they had 12 hours to each day). They could do much better than this because what we would might call 1.1319444 days, would to them have been 1 day, 3 hours and 10 minutes. Since they also invented the second of time (even though it would have been difficult for them to measure a second of time in reality) they arrived at a place beyond which any further splitting of numbers was unnecessary for their needs. What is more, they could achieve a high degree of accuracy in their mathematical calculations.

Had it been possible for them to accurately define the sidereal year, they could have defined it as being equal to 365 days, 3 hours, 4 minutes and 36 seconds. This would have meant their figures were accurate to 0.48 of a second in the whole sidereal year. There is no evidence that they ever did this, because it is virtually certain they could not have ascertained the true length of the sidereal year even if they could have contemplated its existence.

As we have seen, the Sumerians and Babylonians never went beyond assessing the year to be 365.25 days in length. What is more, because they dealt with the 'part of a day' by adding an extra month to the civil calendar every 6 years or so, the civil calendar and the solar calendar were adrift for most of the time. I also mentioned previously that because of their unique non-seasonal climate, for several thousand years the Egyptians got along with a year of 365 days.

Even to achieve the degree of accuracy they did, it was necessary for the Sumerians and the Egyptians to write things down. This alone set them apart from what we would generally refer to as illiterate, and therefore more primitive, peoples who inhabited the world at the same time.

Writing carries many benefits. It is extremely useful in a day-to-day sense, for example when it comes to recording what crops have been grown in any specific district, or to keep track of the number of workers used on a particular building project. Writing also serves to catalogue events so that future generations can understand what their ancestors achieved. This was so important to the Ancient Egyptians that successive pharaohs were not above removing testaments carved into stone by their earlier counterparts and replacing them with versions of history that suited their own purposes better. Writing can also be used to pass on aspects of laws, mythology and religion. In this sense it can be, and usually has been, used as a means of the subjugation of the masses by a literate minority. Even in comparatively recent times in Europe the religious and civil leaders were clearly very worried at the thought of ordinary people learning to read and fought to prevent such an eventuality.

In the past it was generally accepted that the invention and use of writing was one of the hallmarks of true civilization, though this is by no means always the case. For example, although significant knowledge has been amassed regarding what is known as the Indus Valley civilization, which flourished for centuries in what is today India and Pakistan, there is still no real evidence that they had or used a written language and yet nobody would doubt that this was a truly great civilization. Some cultures worthy in every other respect of the title of civilizations in North and South America had no known written language and there are other examples from many different parts of the world.

To historians, any sort of civilization without writing can only be partially understood. We have seen that the period between the Mycenaeans and the Ancient Greeks has been known and in some quarters is still referred to as a 'dark age' and yet there is good evidence that many different parts of Greece were flourishing at this time. What is missing is not culture or civilization, but writing from which experts can gain knowledge of how groups of people were structured and what they knew. The same is broadly true of the more recent European Dark Age, which followed the retreat of the Roman legions from large parts of Western Europe and the arrival of new, warlike people, such as the Franks and the Anglo-Saxons. Written Latin did survive during this period but was lost to large areas of Europe for several centuries. Once again, Western Europe was replete with thriving cultures during this period – it's simply that without writing we know much less about them.

In non-literate societies everything associated with culture, law, religion and so much else depends upon human memory. Oral culture is not so much different than its literate counterpart in that information depends upon a relatively small elite. In a complex oral culture specific individuals would be trained from a very early age to memorize everything necessary to the successful running of a society. This might seem relatively primitive in comparison with libraries of written information

169

but in fact it can be very successful. With billions of neurons and connections in every human brain, the amount an individual can remember is colossal, and all the more so if the mind is conditioned properly and if the information is presented in a form that can be readily accessed in the future.

This might work extremely well for the people concerned but is something of a disaster to historians and archaeologists. Obviously, when a culture such as that of the Ancient Egyptians ceased to exist, it left behind it innumerable records on stone and papyrus, which allow us to know so much about what people did, thought and believed. The same is true in the case of Mesopotamia, where mountains of baked-clay tablets, with their cuneiform writing give us direct access into a long-lived and complex series of cultures. Later, although much of the initial writing and observations of the Ancient Greeks was destroyed through war or the ravages of time, much of what was committed to the written word at the time passed to other cultures and other languages – so it is still available to us today.

Because of a lack of writing in large parts of the ancient world, we know almost nothing about the people who resided in the far west of Europe – right up until the advent of the Roman Empire. The thoughts, aspirations, laws and beliefs of the many hundreds of thousands of people that left us the incredible stone monuments of Britain, France, Central Europe and the Mediterranean region remain almost totally unknown. Even when a tiny part of these related cultures did establish a written language in Minoan Crete, we still cannot understand what they wrote because we have no idea of the language they spoke – and so for the present Linear A might as well not exist.

What we do have is tantalizing glimpses into what was clearly a much more cohesive European population than was ever previously considered to be the case. Advances in genetic testing are beginning to demonstrate how much people moved around, whilst archaeology is showing just how much trade was taking place and how much commonality there was, right back to the Stone Age. Whilst other experts strive to learn what these ancient people ate, how they farmed and the way they lived, it has fallen to me and a very few diehard colleagues to rebuild what they 'knew'. And even despite the fact that the pre-Indo-Europeans of the area seem to have lived within a very different sort of culture to those of Egypt, Mesopotamia or even Ancient Greece, it is becoming obvious that they were in possession of astronomical and mathematical knowledge that, had it been committed to the written word, would have positively eclipsed anything that followed it for almost four thousand years.

It is still generally accepted that the astronomical, and at least some of the geometric, knowledge possessed by the Ancient Greeks had come from further east, particularly from Babylon. This view carries an implication that prehistoric Europe had no legacy of its own, which was as old, if not older, than Mesopotamian civilization. As I intend to demonstrate, such a view is a fallacy.

## Chapter 12

# The Forgotten Ones

As a general rule of thumb, historically it has been the case that if empires are to survive and flourish, they also have to expand. In no case was this more obvious than with the Roman Empire, which, starting from a single city state in Italy, eventually encompassed most of Western Europe and large parts of North Africa. Inevitably, the rising fortunes of any given empire come at the expense of the people it conquers. This is especially true if the people in question relied on an oral transmission of their history, religion and culture. Never was this truer than in the case of the Romans and the inhabitants of the far west of Europe.

When the most famous of all the leaders of Ancient Rome, Julius Caesar, decided the time was right to expand the borders of the Roman Empire, he set his sights on Gaul, a huge area more or less covered by the present boundaries of France. Caesar and his legions marched into the unknown, and even more so when they crossed the English Channel and landed in the south of the British Isles in 55 BC. The lands he sought to conquer were inhabited by a series of tribes, both large and small, all of which were composed of people we have come to call Celts.

The Celts were an intensely warlike people – farmers who had migrated at the start of the Iron Age from the region of Austria and Switzerland. To the Romans, the Celts were clearly savages. They frequently fought amongst themselves, often naked and with their bodies covered in blue dye; the Celts had no written language, no monumental buildings, cities or even large towns and most Celts, even tribal chiefs, lived in wooden and mud round houses. The Celts were great drinkers of beer – and even wine when they could trade for it; though they were fearless fighters, their warfare was haphazard and utterly dependent on individual warriors. In short, despite their bravery and tenacity, they were no real match for the organized Romans and, thinking them so primitive, the Romans considered the Celts perfect for subjugation.

In truth, the picture the Romans painted of Celtic civilization was grossly distorted. Celtic society was advancing, even as Rome began to forge its empire. By the time Caesar made footfall in Britain, some of the tribes there were already developing fairly complex infrastructures. Some minted and used money, and across the Celtic homelands generally, this was certainly not a lawless society. It wasn't in Julius Caesar's best interests to paint the Celts in glowing colours but even in his own writings he pointed out that the illiterate Celts possessed an intellectual component. Caesar made reference to a group within Celtic society that he called 'Druids'. The Druids were odd in terms of the fiercely tribal structure of the society in which they lived because they were the lawyers, priests and wise men whose influence crossed all boundaries and whose representatives were obeyed everywhere, without question.

Caesar tells us that individual Druids were extremely wise and well versed in the traditions, religion and knowledge of their people. Each individual could train for 20 years in order to become an acknowledged Druid, a training that was partly undertaken in specific 'colleges' located throughout the Celtic homelands. Druids were great singers, storytellers and much-revered priests of what was a very complex Celtic religion. In times of inter-tribal conflict Druids would arbitrate and could often bring an end to unnecessary bloodshed because their opinions were both respected and considered binding. Throughout the whole of Celtic society it was a crime punishable by instant death to lay an aggressive finger on any Druid and even to argue with one was considered a serious offence. However, despite the presence of the knowledgeable Druids, the Celts had not developed writing.

It is important to understand that the Celts in Britain and France were not related to the people of the late Stone Age and Bronze Age who had built Stonehenge, Avebury, the stone rows in Carnac or indeed any of the earthworks or stone structures that typified the Megalithic period. In racial terms the Celts were closer to their conquerors, the Romans, because they were Indo-European people, whose ancestors had first entered Europe around 2000 BC. All the same, it is a strange conquering race that takes nothing or learns nothing from the beliefs, abilities or attributes of the peoples it subdues. In reality there is a certain observable continuity in the fringes of Europe during the Iron Age that might indicate the Celts did indeed absorb at least something from extant cultures that had their roots in the pre-Indo-European peoples of Europe.

The Celts certainly appeared to have revered some of the great Megalithic monuments, which were already extremely ancient by the start of the Iron Age. In parts of Britain and Ireland it is quite common to see Iron Age burial mounds grouped together with those of the much earlier Megalithic period, and Iron Age burials or cremations are also fairly common in association with standing stone circles or stone rows and avenues. The motivation behind this apparent reverence for the ancient structures can only be guessed at but it is surely safe to say that the Celts, as different as they may have been in many ways from their forerunners, had a healthy respect for their religion and 'magic'.

Is it also possible that the Celts, mixing with and undoubtedly also mating with the people already in Britain when they arrived, took on board some of the social structures of the earlier society – of which the Druids may have been a significant part? I am not the only researcher to count such a possibility as being extremely likely. Can we see in the scattered farming communities of the British and French Celts a reflection of that much earlier society and also recognize, in the institutions of the Celts, a clue as to the ways in which Megalithic society might have run?

There is little evidence from the Megalithic period of the fierce loyalty Celts owed to their own individual clans and tribes. The late Stone Age and the first part of the Bronze Age seem to have been a relatively peaceful time in the western fringes of Europe. In this respect the Iron Age Celts differed from their earlier counterparts, but the peripatetic priesthood that was the Druids seems likely to have been a notable survivor of a bygone age.

Without a mechanism such as the Druids, Celtic society was so aggressive that it would undoubtedly have torn itself to pieces. Prior to the Roman invasions, Celtic tribes did fight their own wars, one against another, but these were probably diminished by the influence of the Druids, who were respected and obeyed by everyone. Without written evidence we can never know for certain just *how* influential and powerful the Druids were, but the Romans clearly thought they were a force to be feared. Upon arriving in Britain for the real conquest, nearly a century after Julius Ceasar and during the reign of the emperor Claudius, the Roman legions wasted little time before setting off up through what is now Wales, to confront what they considered to be the centre of British Druid power on the island of Anglesey. The sacred groves and settlements of Druids found there were ruthlessly exterminated in what even Romans at the time acknowledged to be a bloodbath. The legions were so intent on this strategy that they left the south of England inadequately garrisoned and as a result nearly lost Britain to attacks made in the south by the rebellious Celtic tribes from East Anglia. Such a disastrous situation could not have come about unless the Romans genuinely considered the Druids to be a threat and were intent on destroying them as soon as possible.

The reader will recall that Professor Alexander Thom found the Megalithic yard to be present in Megalithic structures from the very north of Scotland right down to Brittany in France. There are also indications that it existed much further afield at one time. A very old Spanish unit of measurement, known as the 'vara', which is still used in parts of Latin America and in Texas, because of Spanish influence there, bears a striking resemblance to the Megalithic yard. In addition, the Minoans used a closely related measurement – the Minoan foot. Since there is no evidence that such a widespread population ever constituted a single, cohesive civilization in the late Stone Age or the first part of the Bronze Age, there had to be some common factor that allowed this very precise unit of measurement to be used across such a wide geographical area. The existence of a group such as the Druids, who could cross boundaries and were respected by all the peoples of Western Europe – even extending to the Eastern Mediterranean – seems to be the only explanation for this state of affairs.

Together with Christopher Knight I presented strong evidence in our book *Before the Pyramids*[3] that the Megalithic priesthood had travelled even further than the confines of Europe, as far as Egypt. This is because the arrangement and measurements of the three major pyramids on the Giza Plateau in Egypt are closely related to what was once a very large and very early Megalithic site in North Yorkshire, England. Since the site in Yorkshire was created as early as 3500 BC and the pyramids were not started until after 2000 BC, it stands to reason that the relationship of the two sites must have come from west to east and not the other way around. However, it may not be that this original intellectual priesthood necessarily developed in the far west of Europe. There was a time, not so many decades ago, when most historians would have assumed that the Megalithic builders of Europe could never be dated further back than around 2500 BC. It is now quite apparent that the henges, upon which later stone circles were often based, were created at least 5,500 years ago, but stone structures have a far older pedigree still.

At Göbekli Tepe, in Anatolia, Turkey, is one of the most extraordinary and surprising sites ever excavated by archaeologists. Extending back to at least 11000 BC, the people that ultimately created the mound that Göbekli Tepe now

---

3   Christopher Knight and Alan Butler, *Before the Pyramids*, Watkins, 2011.

represents built a large number of very complex structures in stone. Considerable communal effort must have gone into quarrying and moving the massive stones involved, which were beautifully shaped and smoothed. The site has many large 'T'-shaped stones, some weighing between 10 and 20 tonnes, arranged is such a way as to suggest originally roofed structures. The massive stones carry many expertly created carvings, mostly of wild animals, and it has been suggested that the pillars themselves were also originally intended to represent gods.

Göbekli Tepe is so old that it was certainly commenced before the advent of farming and so must have been created by hunter-gatherers. Nowhere else in the world has such complex and demanding architecture been made by people who were utterly reliant on a pre-agricultural economy. Experts generally agree that the mass of structures on the site, of which only about 5 per cent have been excavated up to now, could not have been created without the prescence of a powerful priesthood of some sort to supervise what must have been centuries of activity. It probably took as many as 500 individuals to find, quarry, move and shape the stones that comprise some of the larger structures, which are up to 30 metres in diameter. The very existence of Göbekli Tepe challenges all previous ideas about what comprises a culture or even a civilization and of course it predates the advent of the Indo-European races by many thousands of years.

Did the people of Göbekli Tepe – and perhaps those of the astonishing nearby Neolithic city of Çatalhöyük, which, although at least two thousand years younger than Göbekli Tepe, is still fantastically old – eventually move west, entering Europe? It is thought likely that farming was first developed in this region of Turkey and it is tempting to think that this new and quite revolutionary form of subsistence would have given the creators of these sites a distinct advantage over hunter-gatherers that they may have encountered in Europe.

An indication that this might have been the case comes from the island of Malta, and more especially from its companion island of Gozo, located in the Mediterranean, not far south of Italy. On Gozo are to be found the Ġgantija temples, structures that were commenced as early as 3600 BC. The site represents two separate temples, built side by side. Once again, monumental stones were used in their construction. Both temples are clover leaf in shape and they contain the truncated remains of huge female statues, depicting extremely portly women with much enhanced breasts and bellies. It was around the time the Ġgantija temples were being commenced in Gozo that the first henges were being laid out in the British Isles and France. Stone working on any scale did not appear in the far west until slightly later, but by 3200 BC monumental stones were being used as far west as Ireland, in the construction of huge passage tombs such as Newgrange.

The stone structures of the Ancient Egyptians, although much more famous, were newcomers on the ground because some of the European passage graves and certainly most of the henges, had already existed for well over a thousand years.

None of these incredible feats of engineering, some of which go far back into the Stone Age, were created by literate cultures and many of them definitely have an astronomical purpose. At the same time as Göbekli Tepe was taking shape in Turkey, Egypt was producing its own Megalithic structures, though these may or may not have something to do with the much later civilization of Ancient Egypt.

Way out in the western deserts of Egypt is the site of Nabta Playa. Here there are deliberately placed standing stones, and even a stone circle, that may have been associated with a culture living in the area as early as the 10th century BC. These people were most probably pastoralists, living at a time when the region was far more fertile and received much more rainfall than it does today. There is no doubt that the stone circle at Nabta Playa had astronomical functions of a fairly high order. Being probably up to six thousand years older than any comparable site in the far west of Europe, the stone builders of Nabta Playa and the surrounding area had plenty of time to migrate into Europe when their own land began to deteriorate and the desert started to encroach.

All of this demonstrates that there were advanced cultures living across a wide area of Europe, western Asia and northern Africa long before the Indo-European era and also several millennia prior to the appearance of the ancient civilizations with which we are most familiar. Many of these people achieved great feats in astronomy and engineering but left us nothing in the way of writing. The inference must be that they were passing on their knowledge and skill via oral traditions and most probably the constant training of a deliberately created priesthood, which undoubtedly perpetuated for centuries.

It has been suggested that the advent of writing and its now almost universal use, though allowing access to a mass of information, has actually made each of us less adept in terms of our memories. At the most mundane level, we often compile a shopping list on some scrap of paper, rather than committing our needs to memory. Children at school are now much less likely to learn long poems as had once been the custom: my father, even at a very advanced age, could recite from memory extremely long poems he had learned as a relatively small child. My guess is that human beings can remember just as much these days as they ever could – the difference is that in a world filled with prompts and with writing we simply don't bother. Ten years ago (slightly unkindly) I wrote a stage play that was two hours in length, in which only one actor took part. Despite what must have seemed like a form of cruelty on my part, the actor in question was soon word perfect, performing the play time and again, flawlessly.

Once, when I was attending an international festival of folk music and storytelling in Wales, I came across a young Zulu man, who was the son of a chief. In conversation with him I learned that, as he would one day inherit the rank of chief from his father, it had been his duty, from early childhood, to learn everything possible about his heritage and ancestors. Together with other interested parties, we persuaded our new friend to recite the verses he had learned, which he managed to do in translation from his own tongue, so that we could understand what he was saying.

What he produced was a series of verses, each one dealing with an ancestor. It started with his father, then followed his paternal line back in time, generation by generation. In each case there was a potted biography of the person in question, with any distinguishing features, information about their lives and details of their achievements, etc. With our encouragement the poem went on and on, certainly for upwards of an hour. Someone was keeping a tally of the number of generations involved and, allowing for a reasonable generational gap, it appeared that the Zulu's story probably went back as far as the 16th century. Even with the aid of genealogical records and computer technology, and after a great deal of effort, I don't know anywhere near as much about my paternal lineage as he did, and yet every part of his story was committed to memory alone.

The fact is that there appears to be virtually no limit to the amount of information we can store in our brains, just as long as it is presented in a memorable way. For example, Aratus' description of the heavens in the *Phaenomena*, mentioned in a previous chapter and taken from the work of Eudoxus, runs to 732 verses and in English is about 7,300 words in length. My play about King Richard III was twice this length, at about 14,000 words and it was learned and performed by a single actor, so it would be easily within the scope of any reasonably intelligent individual to learn the *Phaenomena* of Aratus. Once they had done so and were familiar with its contents, they would have a good understanding of the sky and its major constellations, as well as the way it appeared to change each night and throughout the year.

In our book *Civilization One*, Christopher Knight and I explained in detail how the Megalithic system of measurement had been constructed and how its basic unit of length, the Megalithic yard, could be easily recreated, wherever it was needed. The procedure amounted to a few quite simple instructions and required only a few long wooden stakes, a simple pendulum and a knowledge of the cycles of the planet Venus. Every person that carried out this procedure was not only creating the absolute length of the Megalithic yard, but was also locking into what was surely the most useful and accurate integrated measuring system ever created. Not that the individual concerned needed to know that this was the case. A student priest could have carried out the procedure well, without any knowledge of its ultimate implications.

Also in *Civilization One* we showed how the Sumerian unit of measure, the kush, had been created in more or less the same way, again using a simple pendulum and observing the cycles of Venus. In both cases, gathering together the information 'behind' each system may have taken countless generations of painstaking observation and effort – but the reproduction and testing of its basic premise relied on simple instructions that anyone could have learned in minutes.

When information is broken down into bite-sized units – especially if it is integrated into a poem or a song – it can be stowed away in a human mind for many decades, and emerge as bright, fresh and accurate as it was in the first place.

The best evidence to be found of Megalithic culture comes from the lands bordering the western seaboard of Europe and into the Mediterranean. As Alexander Thom realized decades ago, many of the most significant Megalithic structures, especially in Scotland, are within sight of the sea or sea lochs. We find evidence of Megalithic culture throughout Britain and Ireland, in Brittany, southern Spain and northern Africa. It is to be found on many of the islands of the Mediterranean and as far east as Turkey. What most of the locations in question have in common is close access to the sea. We saw earlier how patterns in trade, right back to the Stone Age, are proving to be more complex and significant than was once thought and we know from fortunate archaeological finds, especially in Britain, that by the Bronze Age seamanship had reached a much more advanced level than anyone would once have suspected.

Even sailors who stick mainly to coastal waters require a good understanding of tides, which can be predicted by the position and movements of the Moon. If they are to remain safe and to navigate successfully, they also require a good knowledge of the major constellations and of how these change the way they appear throughout the night during different seasons.

Whilst Sumer and Egypt had expert boatman with a good knowledge of river navigation, neither were maritime nations. In Mesopotamia civilization developed on land between and surrounding the great rivers Tigris and Euphrates, whilst in Egypt everything about the civilization from beginning to end was inextricably linked to the river Nile. The needs of these two great cultures were radically different than those of peoples whose whole ability to get about relied absolutely on a knowledge of celestial navigation.

From the Stone Age onwards travelling across the heavily wooded, bog-laden wastes of Western Europe was extremely difficult, fearfully laborious and very dangerous. Even beasts of burden were unavailable, let alone useable roads or wheeled vehicles to pass along them. Absolutely everything that passed overland had to be carried by people and in an age when heavy commodities such as flint, salt, copper and bronze were required by communities that did not possess them, only sea and river transport offered a solution.

In which case it was surely absolute necessity that encouraged a growing understanding of the heavens, of how the Moon kept its cycles and the Sun marked out the days and the seasons of the year. Such knowledge might be useful to farmers but was a matter of life and death to anyone regularly going to sea. The same small but very seaworthy cargo ships that plied the waters around Britain and Ireland, and which travelled back and forth along the Mediterranean and up into the Greek islands, would also have carried members of the priesthood, who were respected and consulted by a large number of the inhabitants of maritime Western Europe. Farming societies that also traded extensively became more prosperous; a surplus of food and commodities offered the chance of specialization, in which a very specific group such as these pre-Celtic Druids could have been fed, clothed and supported. Their understanding of the natural world, their knowledge of common weights and measures and surely their understanding of religion and law was the glue that allowed trade to take place and meant that thinly spread people across great distances could retain a commonality.

It would appear that, like the Druids of the much later Celtic peoples, the priests of the late Stone Age and Bronze Age had specific locations at which new members of their fraternity were trained and where new discoveries were made and new knowledge disseminated. They seem to have been especially well represented in the Orkney Islands, off the north coast of Scotland, and also in the north of Yorkshire, in northern England, where the giant henges still to be seen across the landscape were the experimental observatories upon which so much of later Megalithic culture depended. They doubtless supervised the planning and building of huge structures such as Stonehenge and Avebury and officiated in the religious practices that took place in these temples of stone. Members of the British and Continental branches of this Druidic class doubtless visited counterparts on the Mediterranean islands and even ventured as far as Egypt, to confer with its priests and to impart their astronomical and mathematical skills.

It is difficult, if not impossible, to envisage how the Megalithic system of measurement could ever have been developed or have been disseminated across such a vast area unless this form of priesthood had existed, which leads one to wonder: if these people were really so bright, why did they not develop and use writing?

Could it be that they had maintained their traditions for so long they never saw the need for a written language, or might they have deliberately avoided developing and using one? In any age, knowledge is power, but a look at the modern world demonstrates that power structures lose much of their influence once the mass of a population has access to education – and in particular to a knowledge of the written word. The farsighted pre-Celtic Druids may have reasoned that oral transmission kept knowledge exclusive and by so doing afforded them their unique position in the societies they served.

We could envisage a situation in which, generation after generation, the brightest children were taken at an early age and committed to something that can only be equated with much later monasticism. Gradually, and in a specifically created environment, they would have begun to learn the information they would need to carry on the priesthood in their turn. In their isolated colleges they would learn all about astronomy and become experts in celestial navigation. Everything needed, perhaps extending to many hundreds of thousands of words, would eventually be memorized. Much of this knowledge could have been committed to verse or even to song.

There are parallels with the Aboriginal people of Australia, who have inhabited their ancestral lands for countless thousands of years and use such a system to find their way around the massive extent of Australia. Using what are known as 'song lines' these hunter-gatherers have long been able to traverse huge distances in their search for food and game. Each song relates to a journey, and in many cases also relates to the starry patterns of the sky. The song is sung during the long walk from one place to another in an often barren landscape and directions are indicated at certain points in the song –

judged from aspects of the landscape, such as significant hills or even natural depressions in the ground. This method was used to accurately cross an entire continent and the songs are still being taught to a modern generation of Aboriginal children. Even the cadence of the song is important, with clues as to direction being indicated by pitch as well as by lyrics.

Knowledge of the sky and of the various components of the Megalithic system could have been passed on across many generations during the late Stone Age and the Bronze Age in exactly the same way – together with aspects of common law, religious practices, medicine and any amount of other information that set the priesthood apart and made it extremely special – if not appearing magical – and all without a single word being written.

This is a system that can and has worked wonderfully but it does have one major drawback. Once the cohesion of closely related peoples across a vast area began to break down, due to a massive influx of more aggressive and very different sorts of people, the priestly caste itself would have begun to fall apart. Just as surely as the Romans were intent on destroying the Druids of the Celts, so the influx of Indo-Europeans would have dealt a severe blow – even if not a fatal one – to the old ways of disseminating information across the priesthood.

Elements of the age-old knowledge would gradually be lost, whilst the true significance of some of the story cycles would be distorted out of all recognition. What would eventually be left would be shadows of what had once been invaluable information, though it is amazing how long these can remain in place.

In the small northern English town where I lived as a young adult I once overheard old men talking about their own childhood and they referred to the times in winter when they played in the 'dubb'. I had a suspicion I might know what this was, so I asked them what the dubb was. They told me it meant 'puddles' or 'dirty water'. I had previously lived for a while in Wales, so I knew that in Welsh dubb meant 'black' and that Welsh children referred to puddles as 'dubb glass', which means black water. The Welsh language has not been spoken in the north of England for upwards of 1,500 years, and yet elements of it had managed to survive amongst the Germanic-speaking Anglo-Saxons, where in this case it had become slang, used only by children.

This same echo of the past regarding the Megalithic system of measurements definitely did exist because many of the measures used in the British Isles up until the very recent decimalization (and still favoured extensively now) are directly attributable to the system. These include the pound of weight and the pint of volume, but also many other fairly obscure units that are no longer used.

Perhaps the original priesthood continued, existing 'underground', with at least some knowledge passed on through specific families and kept secret from society as a whole – even to the extent that the people themselves lost much of the original sense of what they so carefully learned at their parent's knees.

Certainly enough clues have been left behind, both in terms of modern units and thanks to archaeological discoveries, to allow us to recreate the system of knowledge in its original form, though it is likely to be some time before orthodox historians accept that pre-literate cultures from such a remote period could actually have been as clever as we are today.

## Chapter 13

# A New Understanding

Just as we generally like our homes and surroundings to be neat and tidy – to have a plan for our lives and to live in an ordered society – we also seem to need to treat history in the same way. This is fairly easy to achieve when it comes to the recent past because, after all, we have a great deal of written evidence at our disposal. In much of Western Europe this proves to be the case as far back as the expansion of the Roman Empire. Although Roman accounts are inevitably skewed in favour of the conquerors, we know in what year expansions were made, when uprisings against the Romans took place, which emperor replaced his predecessor and when, and how and at what period the Roman Empire began to fall to pieces.

This is all possible because the Romans had a written language and possessed writers whose self-appointed task was to document every aspect of Roman civilization, conquest and rule. As the Roman Empire began to contract, broadly speaking in the 5th and 6th centuries, things become difficult again for the historian, until writing once again became the norm as new nation states began to be created throughout the previously occupied parts of Western Europe.

The Romans themselves had taken nearly everything they knew of history, art and culture from Ancient Greece, which they admired immensely. Unfortunately, the Ancient Greeks were not so lucky. Their culture had sprung from the relative darkness of a history that existed only in myth and legend. They had stories, left over from the earlier Minoan and Mycenaean periods and they also pieced together what they could of their own history by recourse to scribes and priests in Sumer and Egypt, but neither of these cultures was sufficiently ancient to know what had taken place in Europe and indeed in other areas, way back into the Stone Age.

Under such circumstances, our only recourse these days, when it comes to understanding what was taking place across a vast area, over extremely lengthy periods of time, is to rely on archaeology. There is no doubt that archaeology is a science that has advanced in leaps and bounds in recent decades. Innovations such as ground-penetrating radar and various forms of chemical and other dating techniques have revolutionized our ability to open a window on even the very ancient past – but the glass in that window is clouded to say the least.

Generally speaking, archaeology deals mostly in rubbish. This is not intended to be in any way a criticism, as most archaeologists would readily appreciate. Despite our modern striving for order and neatness, we are a very messy species and it is thanks to our ancestors' tendency not to clear up after themselves that we know as much about their lives as we do. The sorts of artifacts that archaeologists discover in places where people once lived tend to be items that were either lost or discarded. In addition, a great deal of evidence is also to be had from the fact that many of our ancestors, across a vast period of time, showed a desire to take some of their most desirable possessions and even fairly mundane domestic objects into the afterlife with them. As a result, burials with their attendant grave goods can be mines of information.

Gradually, and with painstaking detail, records are kept regarding finds from any given culture, leading to a consensus. As a result, we might know, for example, what dimensions Iron Age roundhouses tended to be, the sort of loom weights people favoured to secure their yarn, the kind of food they generally ate and even, on rare and special occasions, what their clothes looked like.

Beyond the minutiae and trash of everyday life in an ancient and pre-literate culture, the sky of knowledge darkens significantly. Archaeologists may excavate something that looks like a ceremonial meeting place or even a temple but without hard evidence it is invariably impossible to know what took place in such locations and, together with so much else, such matters of conjecture are listed under the heading of 'ritual activity'. We might also know how a particular culture tended to dispose of its dead, but we have not the slightest clue as to the beliefs of the individuals concerned or the ceremonies that took place as they were laid to rest.

Archaeologists and their professional associates tend to be amongst the most patient people imaginable – and they are naturally conservative. Their forerunners, the treasure hunters of the 17th and 18th centuries, were quite willing to indulge in the most outrageous speculation – for example, attributing Avebury and other Megalithic sites in Britain and France to the Romans, the Ancient Greeks, the Egyptians or a range of other cultures, none of whom could have been remotely involved in their construction. Modern experts would never dream of jumping to what could turn out to be erroneous conclusions – partly because their careers depend upon care and consistency, but mostly because they have a genuine desire to establish 'the truth'.

This attitude is laudable in one way but it sometimes leads to a tendency to throw out the baby with the bathwater. The best example I can think of is one I mentioned earlier, namely the myth that suggested the stones of Stonehenge had come from the west – in Ireland. As it turns out, this apparently fanciful story is at least *half* true, in that it is now known that the bluestones were brought all the way from west Wales – a staggering distance considering the period and the difficulty of transporting anything of significant size at such an early date.

When it was first suggested by geologists that there was no such stone anywhere near Salisbury Plain, where Stonehenge stands, and that it must have come from Preseli in Wales, there were groans of protest from archaeologists because hardly anyone dreamed that such an epic undertaking would have been possible. As we have seen, some tried to extricate themselves from what seemed like an impossible situation by suggesting that these stones had actually been brought from Wales thousands of years previously by the natural action of glaciers and had been found locally. It has now been demonstrated to the satisfaction of almost everyone that this could not have been the case and that all the bluestones were indeed laboriously manhandled, mostly by coastal and river transport, from many miles to the west.

There is a parallel here with the Megalithic yard, which was unconsciously unearthed by Professor Alexander Thom across decades of measuring Megalithic structures. He wasn't looking for it – it just happened to be there. The reaction of most archaeologists was – and still is – that 'logically the Megalithic yard cannot exist and therefore it does not exist', irrespective of how much evidence Thom's statistics demonstrated. One group of scientists, mathematicians, presented Thom with a specially struck gold medal for his persistence and accuracy in statistics, whilst another group, archaeologists, as good as branded him delusional – a position most still hold. Perhaps this isn't too surprising. Everyone associated with ancient history could see that the implications of a common and very accurate unit of measurement, from such a remote period, across a vast area and surviving for maybe two thousand years, would rewrite ancient history. It would pose far more questions than it might answer. It was easier by far to ignore the Megalithic yard and hope it might conveniently go away.

Unfortunately for Thom's critics this has not been the case. On the contrary, what started out as an isolated and little-understood linear unit has now expanded to become just one feature of an integrated measuring system that dealt with distance, mass, volume and time. Using the evidence acquired from a variety of sources it has proved possible to infer that those who created and used the Megalithic system had acquired it as a result of probably many centuries of investigation into the behaviour of the very sky above their heads. As the great 18th-century American patriot and scientist Thomas Jefferson had pointed out, only the turning Earth was a reliable way of measuring both time and distance, because nothing else in the natural world, and available to a pre-technological culture, was accurate enough or consistent enough to rely upon.

Jefferson (1743–1826), writer of the Declaration of Independence and third President of a free United States, was utterly fascinated by measurements, partly as a result of having been trained as a surveyor by his father. During his lifetime, forms of measurement across the world were diffuse and often wildly inaccurate. This made foreign trade extremely complicated; at a time when science was starting to become both respectable and desirable, it also meant that co-operation between scientists in different countries was awkward.

As Secretary of State, in the mid 1790s, Thomas Jefferson proposed to the American government a completely new form of measurement, based upon the length of a pendulum rod that would swing back or forth in exactly one second of time. His proposal was ingenious, it covered all aspects of measurement and he hoped it would be adopted across the globe.

Jefferson had formerly been the United States ambassador to France, where he had spent several years. Whilst in Paris he had conversed regularly with leading members of the French Academy of Sciences. He had also spent many years looking at historical measuring systems and was clearly very conversant with his subject.

For the first part of his life Jefferson had been a British subject, so quite naturally he had studied British weights and measures most carefully of all. Although he found British weights and measures to have become somewhat haphazard and inconsistent, he did recognize that underpinning them was something that was not only incredibly old, but which had once been extremely self-consistent and very accurate. In other words, he could sense that British length, weight and volume measurements had once been intimately and very cleverly related – but in a way that seemed to belie the mess that measuring had become by his own era.

It was towards the essence of what he saw as having been the 'ultimate' and original European system of measurements that Jefferson wanted to return. Unwittingly, he proposed a method for 'proving' his basic unit of length (i.e. a pendulum) that the Megalithic priests had themselves used.

Perhaps unfortunately, his new system was never adopted. At almost exactly the same time he proposed it to the US government, the French were rolling out their new 'metric' system. This was not based on the length of a pendulum string or rod, but rather on the circumference of the Earth. French explorers and scientists had measured a quadrant of the Earth, from the north pole to the equator, and had split the distance into 1,000,000 units, which they chose to call metres. Mass and volume measures were based on the metre. Unfortunately, they underestimated the size of the polar circumference of the Earth slightly, so the metre, as a millionth part of the quadrant, was wrong from the start. These days the meter is defined by much more accurate means and, as with any measuring system, as long as there is true consistency, everyone can rely on it.

Despite the metric system, provided there was a clock advanced enough to measure one second of time accurately, Jefferson's system would have worked as well, if not better than the metric system. It had the advantage of being checkable by anyone, anywhere – as long as they possessed an accurate clock. This had also been true of the Megalithic system, though in this case the clock was provided by the turning Earth itself, and also by the known and consistent movements of the planet Venus. What was more, the Megalithic yard was derived not simply from a pendulum length but, like the metric system, also related directly, and more accurately, to the polar circumference of the Earth.

We live in a world in which most if not all of the great achievements of history have been attributed to cultures that possessed the written word. In essence, despite the fact that we have now learned a great deal about other ancient civilizations, our society responds as much to classical Greece as did that of the Romans. We take it for granted that the observations of undoubted geniuses such as Pythagoras and Archimedes were attributable entirely to them – or at the very least to the schools and academies that took their names. If we could talk to them now – provided they were sufficiently modest – they would undoubtedly say something similar to the more modern Isaac Newton, who is acclaimed as the father of modern science. When talking about the origin of his own discoveries Newton said 'If I have seen further it is by standing on the shoulders of giants.' In his case the giants in question were most probably Greek, but we should not forget that the classical Greeks were, themselves, the legatees of something far, far older, and perhaps in some ways far cleverer too.

What I am suggesting is that just as surely as even Newton himself was relying on discoveries and observations from the past, so the classical Greeks were not drawing their knowledge from thin air. In amongst the mathematical systems they inherited from their contemporary neighbours, the Sumerians and the Egyptians, the Greeks also had access to something more local and far older. Because this reservoir of peculiarly European knowledge had been based entirely on oral traditions, much of it had been lost during the Indo-European watershed after 2000 BC. Nevertheless, components of it were still present.

Although Greek mathematicians looked east for the form of geometry they used, the zodiac favoured by Greek astronomers was of a type that had clearly come from Crete. The result was a slightly creaky hybrid. In the Cretan (European 366°) system, the Sun had moved at 1° per day within the zodiac, whereas when allied to the Sumerian system it only managed 0.986° per day. In the ancient European system, time measurement and geometry were one and the same thing, mainly because the system had developed with sea-borne navigation in mind.

I will never forget the tremendous insight that was offered to me nearly three decades ago when I read a book entitled *Sky and Sextant* by an American writer, John P Budlong. Mr Budlong was a self-taught navigator, so questions popped into his mind that might not have occurred to an academically taught person. When talking about the mechanisms of oceanic navigation Mr Budlong observed that he wasn't aware who it was that first decided to measure both time and geometry using the terms minutes and seconds, but he was sure that the complications that arise as a result must have cost many lives over the centuries. Mr Budlong was painfully aware that to the modern navigator, time and geometry are far from being the same thing.

This strange state of affairs, which perpetuated until modern technology rescued us from having to do navigational calculations manually, was due to the fact that the Ancient Greeks were relying on a 'hybrid' system, in which geometry and time keeping had become separated. Meanwhile, in the ancient European system, time and geometry were identical, making necessary calculations far easier and much less susceptible to error.

To the modern astronomer, the tortured association between the geometry of the heavens and the passage of time is not really a problem because we live in an age of decimal points. We have to remember that our ancient ancestors did everything they could to avoid splitting numbers, which is why the system of degrees, minutes and seconds developed in the first place.

This peculiar state of affairs, using minutes and seconds to measure time *and* geometry, has perpetuated for well over two thousand years, and is just one example of the evidence that elements of what we came to call the Megalithic system of measurement have survived up to the present day, if we only look for them in the correct places.

We can find the Megalithic system 'frozen' into the gigantic stone structures that still dot the landscapes of Britain, France and other parts of Western Europe. It exists in the fabulous palaces, created by Cretan builders four thousand years ago, as well as within the number matrices upon which the mysterious Phaistos Disc is based. The Megalithic system can be seen behind the glass screens of any delicatessen in the United States of America, or indeed still here in Britain, where shoppers still buy their ham, cheese or any other commodity in Megalithic units of weight. If I lay aside my writing tonight and decide to go out for a drink with friends, I will experience the Megalithic system when I buy a pint of beer because pounds, pints and numerous other examples of British and American weights and measures originally derived from the Megalithic yard.

It has been through comparing these remaining snippets of evidence that it gradually proved possible to recreate the Megalithic system of measurement in its original splendour. The result is something that, if generally accepted, would shake the foundations of ancient history.

Only if we were to stand and listen to the buzz of conversation in some market place, for example in Bilbao or San Sebastián, in the Basque region of Spain, could we hear something like the language of those truly ancient European traders and navigators. Languages similar to Basque existed in other Western extremities of Europe until comparatively recently but have now been superseded by tongues of the Indo-European language family. In the increasingly global community that humanity now represents, other relics of the truly ancient past, such as pounds and ounces, pints and gallons, will also give way to the irrepressible power of the metric system. We cannot stop the march of progress but neither should we consign important components of our past to oblivion, simply because to look at them in detail means rewriting our own history.

Facts have to be faced, no matter how uncomfortable they may be. At least five thousand years ago, in Europe, pre-literate cultures across a vast area were so closely associated that we might, reasonably, refer to them as one 'civilization'. It is very likely that they spoke a common language and held common religious beliefs; they traded extensively across huge areas, were expert navigators and they somehow created the most accurate and yet the simplest integrated measuring system the world has ever known.

Being drawn directly from the motion of the turning Earth, this system of measuring distance, mass, volume and time was based upon a staggeringly accurate assessment of the polar circumference of the Earth. It was certainly present as early as 3500 BC and it endured until it was gradually lost after around 1500 BC. Its demise was undoubtedly due to a dislocation of its long-standing motivating force – a revered and learned priesthood, the influence of which can be detected from the furthest western shores of Europe, throughout the Mediterranean and into North Africa.

The Indo-Europeans, who had begun their own journey far to the east, maybe as far away as Central Asia, entered Europe around 2000 BC. The first civilizations of worth that they encountered were those of the Egyptians and the Sumerians, from whom they eventually learned much of their astronomy, geometry and mathematics. Only later, as the migrations continued, did the Indo-Europeans come into contact with a very different form of civilization. Their very presence and diffusion broke down the bonds of the older, extended civilization in areas of Western Europe. The priesthood was dislocated, destroyed or subsumed, so that its unique way of looking at and measuring the world was, to a great extent, lost.

Despite its entirely oral tradition, elements of this ancient knowledge did survive. It perpetuated in places of trade and commerce, where people were reluctant to abandon weights and measures upon which their survival depended. Units such as the pound and the pint represent an incredible bridge between us and that remote period but the unit of length upon which everything was based, the Megalithic yard, gradually disappeared from use. The Megalithic unit of length that did survive was the foot. It is utterly incredible to realize that the statute foot, still used regularly in Britain and almost exclusively in the United States, differs from the ultimately Megalithic Minoan foot by only 1mm. It carries an unfortunate name, because although it approximates the length of an average male foot, it was originally derived, like the Megalithic yard, from the polar circumference of the Earth. It is merely a more convenient variant of the Megalithic yard because there are exactly 1,000 Minoan feet to 366 Megalithic yards.

Geographically speaking, the Ancient Greeks occupied a unique position. The area was heavily affected by the Indo-European incursions but at the same time it owed a great deal of its cultural past to the Bronze Age Mycenaean culture, which in turn had derived much of its knowledge from the

Minoans. The astonishing Antikythera Mechanism shows aspects of both influences. It relied on mathematics that the Greeks took from the Babylonians, and therefore ultimately the Sumerians, but was based upon a version of astronomy that came from Crete and which was therefore of a wholly prehistoric European origin. The Antikythera Mechanism is therefore representative of a somewhat awkward amalgam of knowledge, and despite its staggering degree of engineering competence from such a very early time, it is, as we have seen, not especially accurate in its astronomical predictions.

From almost two thousand years earlier comes the Phaistos Disc, which, although not representing the engineering skill of the Antikythera Mechanism, does display a purely European view of astronomy, geometry and mathematics. As an aide-memoire to the Megalithic system it works flawlessly. Had the Megalithic system not fragmented around the time of the Indo-European arrivals and if the classical Greeks had therefore been able to adopt it in its original form, it is quite possible that we would still be relying on it totally today. As it is, there are only echoes of the Megalithic system still to be found at work in the world. The ounce and the pound, the pint, the gallon and the statute foot, although not officially sanctioned any more in Great Britain, are used on a daily basis all over the United States. How long this continues is surely in some doubt because the metric system is already the lingua franca of the scientific world.

It doesn't matter too much what or which measuring system the world chooses to use henceforth. Just as long as everyone is reading from the same hymn sheet and provided the measurements are accurate and fully checkable, things will carry on successfully. What might be a pity would be to lose touch with something from our remotest past that is truly extraordinary. It should be fully studied and preserved now, before its last vestiges disappear from daily use altogether. Fortunately, in a way this is happening, even without the acknowledgement of supposed experts that such a people and such an incredible, fully integrated system of mathematics, geometry, astronomy and terrestrial measurement ever existed.

For as long as the hot Mediterranean sun rises over the magnificent ruins of Knossos and Phaistos in Crete, and while the gaunt and weathered stone circles of the far west of Europe keep their lonely vigils over the chalk grasslands and upland heather of the British Isles and Brittany, we will have access to that extraordinary, early flowering of human ingenuity and the dawn of genius.

*Appendix One*

# The Phaistos Disc and Measuring the Year

## Why does the Length of the Year Matter?

If the Earth was more obliging in the way it orbits the Sun, the length of the year wouldn't really matter at all. If it took the Earth exactly 365 days to go around the Sun, instead of 365.2564 days, there would be no problem, but the fact that it doesn't has been an irritant to people for just about as long as we have been around. The reason is straightforward. It's impossible to have part of a day in a year. If we considered the year to have 365 days, that's too short, and if we celebrate a year of 366 days, that would be too long. Either way, if we don't make some sort of compensation, things will soon start to go wrong – for all sorts of people.

In any culture that has taken to farming, the calendar is very important. Farmers need to know, from year to year, when to plant their crops and to carry out all the other necessary tasks with regard to crops and animals. If no compensation is made for the 365.2564-day year, dates on the calendar will begin to slip back through the year – by roughly one day every four years. It doesn't sound much of a problem but it soon adds up. Within a few generations, Easter becomes Christmas, summer becomes spring and nobody has any idea what they should be doing, or when.

Fishermen and sailors need accurate calendars too. In any place on the planet there are times in the year when it is safe to sail and other periods when it would definitely be best to stay at home. Once again, without an accurate judgement of the date, the accumulated wisdom of generations is worth nothing.

## Making Compensations

Being the ingenious creatures we are, humanity has dealt with this problem in a number of different ways. Some cultures, such as the Sumerians and the Babylonians, decided on a year judged by the orbits of the Moon. That's fine in some ways, but it doesn't address the problem of the number of days in the year. From full Moon to full Moon is 29.53 days – another very unhelpful number. And since 29.53 does not divide into 365.2564, in some ways it makes matters even worse. In the end these cultures settled for a year of 360 days. They knew this wasn't right, so they compensated by adding an extra month to the calendar every six years or so. It more or less worked and the 360 days became the basis of geometry, but, although they didn't know it, the Sumerians and the Babylonians were storing up difficulties for later.

The Egyptians had a year of 365 days. Actually their year was 360 days but they added an extra 5 days 'off' the calendar each year. This meant they were always a quarter of a day wrong but

Egypt had unique needs. Although it was a farming culture, the seasons didn't matter to Egypt. Farming in Egypt relied on the time of year when the river Nile flooded. Everything was based on this happening and it was judged in a way that had nothing to do with the length of the year and everything to do with the behaviour of a star named Sirius. As a result the Egyptians muddled along pretty well. They hardly ever sailed in the open sea, so navigation was no problem and they were generally insulated from most of the potential problems of an incorrect year.

# Our Calendar

By the time of Julius Caesar, the Roman calendar was in a hopeless mess. He tried to put things right by making compensations at regular intervals – not unlike the method of correction we use now. Unfortunately his astronomers made a basic error in their calculations, so over a protracted period, things went wrong again. Finally, in the reign of Pope Gregory XIII (1572–85) something had to be done. The modern world adopted the version of the calendar we still use, and because of the pope in question it is still called the Gregorian calendar.

To keep things on track we have to remember a series of different procedures. Every fourth year is a leap year, and an extra day is added to February. In itself this is not enough, so another rule is applied. For example, if a year is divisible by 100, as in the year 1900, we don't add the extra day, but if the year is also divisible by 400, as was the case in the year 2000, we do add it. It is all rather complicated but we live in a technological society and there is always some clever person around who can tell us what to do. So that's the problem solved – or is it?

# The Months

Most historical cultures have celebrated 12 months in a year. The word month comes from the word Moon and, as we have seen, there are roughly 12 full Moon to full Moon cycles in a year, so it's quite sensible to have 12 months in a year. Unfortunately, this doesn't work in terms of making all the months the same length. They can't all have 30 days, because 12 x 30 is 360, which isn't enough, and they can't all be 31 days because 12 x 31 is 372 days, which is too many days for the year. In our culture we have a frightening array of different numbers of days in our months. Once again we have to remember the verse, 'Thirty days hath September, April, June and November. All the rest have 31, save February clear, which has 28 and 29 each leap year.'

Probably the most sensible method would have been to have months alternating between 30 and 31 days. This would almost be correct but it comes to 366 days, which is slightly too long. However, this isn't the only potential problem we face – we have to know what sort of year we want to use.

# The Wrong Sort of Year?

A factor that we haven't so far taken into account is that there is definitely more than one 'sort' of year. The Gregorian calendar is based upon what is known as the 'tropical year'. The easiest way to explain this is by way of the equinoxes. On two days each year, in spring and in autumn, the Sun rises absolutely due east on the horizon. Throughout the rest of the year sunrise takes place either north of east, or south of east, dependent on the season, but on these two specific days, it rises due east and sets due west. These days are known as the spring and autumn equinoxes.

The time between one spring or autumn equinox and the next is 365.2422 days: this is the tropical year and is the one upon which the Gregorian calendar is based. The tropical year is the 'logical' year because it is the one ordinary people can see, but it could be argued that this isn't really the length of the year at all.

The true mark of a year is the time it takes the Earth to orbit the Sun once, and to return to the exact place in space where it started. This sort of year is called a sidereal year and it is slightly longer than a tropical year. The sidereal year is 365.2564 days in length. In effect, there is a 20-minute difference between the two sorts of year.

## Why is There a Difference?

Although everyone these days is aware that the Earth and all the other planets revolve around the Sun, this isn't immediately obvious from an Earth-bound perspective. On the contrary, to anyone standing on the surface of the Earth and looking out into space, it appears as if the Sun, the Moon and all the planets, together with the stars, are revolving around us. Until comparatively recently it was assumed that the Earth was the centre of everything. In order to be able to measure what happens in space, it was necessary for our ancient ancestors to create some sort of reference, so they would know which part of the sky they were looking at, at any time of day or night.

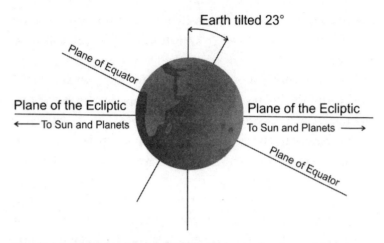

*The Earth is tilted on its axis by 23° relative to the plane of the solar system. From our perspective the Sun, Moon and planets all circle the Earth around what is known as the Plane of the Ecliptic.*

The Sun, Moon and all the planets appear to travel around the Earth in a huge circle and they all keep to the same general track. The path around which they all travel is known as the Plane of the Ecliptic. In order to make sense of it all, our ancestors split the Plane of the Ecliptic into 12 equal sections. They remembered which section was which by looking at the patterns of stars in each section. They made imaginary pictures of the stars and gave names to them. Each section was ruled by one particular group of stars. They thought one of the groups looked like a ram, so they called it Aries, which means Ram. Another they considered had the shape of a bull, so they called that one Taurus, which means bull. All twelve sections of the sky were named in this way. This was the backdrop against which the Moon or any of the planets travelled, so they could be tracked successfully. Taken together, the belt of twelve constellations became known as the 'zodiac'. The Sun appears to travel through the zodiac too but it isn't possible to see which of the zodiac signs the Sun is in, because it is so bright it blots out all the background stars, but people knew from experience what zodiac sign it occupied.

Our view of the sky depends entirely upon the Earth, because that is where we are standing. As it travels through space, the

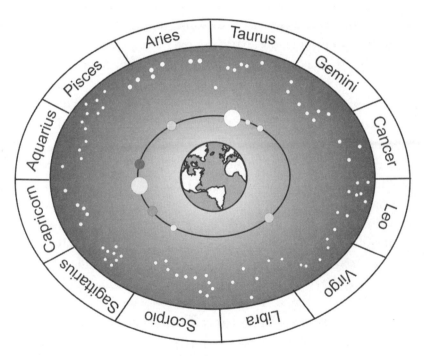

*From the point of perspective of anyone looking out from the Earth, it appears that the Sun, Moon and planets orbit between the Earth and the background stars, as in this graphic. The band of the sky through which they travel is called the zodiac and is split into 12 sections.*

Earth also turns on its own axis, once each day. It also keeps to a particular angle relative to the Sun, which is around 23°. However, the Earth behaves something like a child's spinning top. Not only does the Earth turn on its own axis, it also 'wobbles'. This is a fairly complicated business, but suffice it to say that one whole wobble takes an incredible 26,000 years! This wobble causes a gradual but definite alteration in the way we see the sky. What it effectively means is that, although the Sun at the spring or autumn equinox will always rise due east, it will not always be in the same zodiac sign. The place in the zodiac where spring and autumn equinox happens moves backwards through the zodiac signs very, very slowly.

This is called the 'precession of the equinoxes' and it is what causes the tropical year to be a different length from the sidereal year. The time difference is only 20 minutes each year, but once again it soon adds up, and it causes complications, especially for astronomers, whose job it is to study the sky.

To ordinary people in any culture the difference between the length of the two types of year doesn't matter a fig. The change is so slow that within a human lifetime the equinoxes won't move back by more than a single degree within the zodiac. But such things do matter to astronomers and also to entire civilizations, if those civilizations last a long time.

## How the Minoans Dealt with the Situation

One way to deal with the compensations necessary to regulate the calendar would be to invent some sort of number system that ran alongside a calendar with an even number of days, so that after a definite and prescribed period, a necessary correction would be made to the calendar. The evidence suggests that the Minoans opted for a year of 366 days. They split the year into 12 months, alternating between 30 and 31 days.

Of course this isn't correct and such a calendar would soon run out of sequence with both the tropical and the sidereal year – so how to regulate it, easily and efficiently?

How the Minoans came up with the solution that they ended up using is a mystery. Using two numbers, they managed to create a system that would regulate the 366-day year to either the tropical year or the sidereal year. What the Minoans did, on a year-by-year basis, was incredibly simple, as we will see, but underpinning it is something almost miraculous for a so-called primitive culture.

In essence, the Minoans used what are known as algorithms. An algorithm can be defined as 'a set of rules that precisely defines a sequence of operations'. To correct both the sidereal and the tropical year the Minoans began with a period of 14,637 days. 14,637 is the lowest common denominator of two particular numbers. These numbers are 123 and 119. In other words 123 x 119 = 14,637. The use of these numbers by the Minoans is indicated by the number of hieroglyphs on each side of the Phaistos Disc (see overleaf).

# The Sidereal Year

The Minoans ran a 123-day cycle alongside the 366-day year. After four cycles of 123 days, which is 492 days, they simply skipped a day in the 366-day calendar. (In other words they treated the day as if it had never existed.) They kept on

*Side A of the Phaistos Disc carries 123 symbols.*

*Side B of the Phaistos Disc carries 119 symbols.*

doing this for 119 cycles of 123 days (14,637 days), at the end of which they added three extra days to the 366-day calendar. (As indicated by three dots at the end of side A of the disc.) They then began the procedure all over again. What they ended up with was a year of 365.25625 days, as against the true sidereal year of 365.25636 days. Their system was incorrect by an average of 9 seconds of time per year – which is almost beyond belief, especially considering that no whole number has to be split to achieve the procedure. This version of the sidereal calendar would need no other compensation for almost ten thousand years – which is longer than any civilization has ever lasted. This method is more than 99.9999 per cent accurate.

# The Tropical Year

What is astounding about the method the Minoans used to regulate the year is that they used the same numbers for both the sidereal and the tropical year – but they simply turned them round. In the case of the tropical year they ran a 119-day cycle alongside the 366-day calendar. The procedure in this case was to skip two days in the 366-day calendar after nine cycles of 119 days. No days needed to be added to the end of the 14,637-day period in this case and the procedure just went on and on, with no other correction needed. The year achieved was 365.24167 days, as against the true tropical year of 365.24220 days. In the case of the tropical year, the Minoan method was incorrect by 46 seconds per year. Though not as accurate as the sidereal method, this is still staggering. It means that no other correction to the tropical year would be needed for almost two thousand years, meaning this method is 99.9997 per cent accurate.

As a frame of reference, the modern Gregorian calendar is at odds with the real tropical calendar by 25 seconds per year, which is midway between the accuracy of the two Minoan systems. However, the Minoan system can be used for two different types of year, is simpler to use, with less rules to remember and is four thousand years old!

## Appendix Two

# Tracking the Planets

As we have seen, the ancients – in this case the Minoans – chose to split the great circle of heaven, within which the Sun, Moon and planets orbit, into 12 more or less equal units. This band of stars, which runs around what is known as the Plane of the Ecliptic, is known as the zodiac. The reason this was done was so that it was possible to know where any of the planetary bodies, or the Sun and Moon, were to be found at any given point of time. Although somewhat modified to the needs of modern science, the zodiac constellations are still used as points of reference and many constellations of stars (apparent groups of stars) still retain the names they were given in antiquity.

## The Zodiac Constellations

The twelve zodiac constellations are Aries – the Ram, Taurus – the Bull, Gemini – the Twins, Cancer – the Crab, Leo – the Lion, Virgo – the Virgin, Libra – the Scales, Scorpio – the Scorpion, Sagittarius – the Archer, Capricorn – the Goat, Aquarius – the Water Carrier and Pisces – the Fish.

For the sake of accuracy each of these zodiac constellations would have been split into degrees. To the Minoans, and to the Megalithic peoples, there were undoubtedly either 30° or 31° to each zodiac sign. This matched the number of days in the year and was particularly responsive to the Sun. In the Megalithic system of geometry the Sun can be observed to move at almost exactly 1° per day through the zodiac, which with our present system of geometry it does not. Months were alternately comprised of 30 and 31 days, which perfectly matched the Sun's progression through the zodiac.

In terms of its daily movements, and especially when using the Megalithic system of geometry and time keeping, the Sun is reliable and was easy to track. The Moon, which zips through each of the zodiac signs in a couple of days, is more awkward but the planets of the solar system have very complicated orbits when seen from the Earth. This is mostly because they, like us, are orbiting the Sun, which gives a rather strange perspective when seen from Earth. For example, it is quite possible for any of the planets to sometimes appear to halt their progress through the zodiac and to start moving backwards for a period of time. Of course, nothing of the sort is actually taking place. This is purely a line-of-sight effect, caused by the fact that the Earth itself is orbiting the Sun.

## Planetary Movement

Since all the planets of the solar system take a different amount of time to orbit the Sun, and because our own orbit thoroughly complicates the issue, planet tracking within the zodiac can be a fiercely difficult matter. In addition, the planets Mercury and Venus are closer to the Sun than is the Earth, so when seen from our perspective they never wander too far from the Sun and appear to us, alternatively, as either morning or evening stars. Those planets with orbits further out than the Earth – known as the 'superior' planets – are not restricted in this way and can be viewed at different times in any part of the zodiac.

We might ask why any fairly primitive culture would even have any interest in what the planets of the solar system did, across days, months or years. Initially their interest may simply have been related to the fact that human beings are inherently curious. Planets behave differently than stars and are therefore somewhat mysterious. The fact that their orbits are 'odd' and that they can sometimes even travel backwards, was probably enough incentive for early stargazers to wish to know more about their habits.

Knowing where the planets were was also a matter of religion. All of the planets of the solar system are named after Roman gods: names that were themselves derived from gods and goddesses once revered in Greece. It can be demonstrated that the behaviour of specific planets, across time and in their association with each other, is related to ancient myth cycles about the gods and their attributes. As two examples, Venus, second planet out from the Sun, was also the Roman goddess of love, who to the Greeks was known as Aphrodite. Jupiter, which is by far the largest of the solar system's planets and which is the fifth planet from the Sun, was the king of the gods to the Romans; his Greek name was Zeus.

# Astronomy and Astrology

In all probability, to the Greek or Roman mind the planets were not simply 'representative' of gods and goddesses, they literally *were* them. It therefore made sense to know where one's preferred god or goddess happened to be in the sky at any particular point in time, so that prayers could be directed appropriately. It is equally likely that at least some early observers of the planets and their motions were much more interested in the mathematics of the situation, something that continues until the present day.

Generally speaking there are two different motivations for planet watching these days. The study of astronomy is a purely scientific matter and has nothing whatsoever to do with the myths, legends or religion of the stars and planets. On the other hand, astrology, which still interests many millions of people throughout the world, serves a very different function. Believers in astrology assume that the position of the planets within the zodiac can have a direct bearing on everything that happens here on Earth. Astrologers track the planets carefully. They are interested in the positions the planets have within the zodiac and also the relationship they have to each other, in terms of angles. At its most elevated, astrology suggests that everything taking place on the Earth and within the lives of its inhabitants, is directly related to planetary movement and interaction.

Don't expect to get any sympathy regarding astrology from a modern astronomer. The vast majority of astronomers positively hate astrology and consider it to be nothing but superstitious nonsense. Whether or not astrology has any real credibility, perhaps modern astronomers should show a little more patience. After all, the two studies, astrology and astronomy, were indistinguishable until just a few centuries ago. There was a time, even as recently as the 16th or even the 17th century, when virtually no emperor or king would have embarked on any significant venture unless his astrologers considered the planets were propitious for whatever undertaking was being considered.

The best we can say about the attitude of those who spent their lives gazing at the star-clad heavens in Minoan Crete, or across great swathes of Western Europe, four thousand or more years ago, is that we are unsure regarding their true motivations. It is almost certain that the dividing line between science and religion was so blurred during this long-gone period that their interest was mathematical and devotional in equal proportions.

# Ancient Motivations

What we can nevertheless be sure about is that these ancient peoples went to great trouble to track the planets within the solar system. It is also evident that they sometimes used the knowledge they gained for purely practical purposes. A good instance of this is the fact that the Megalithic yard, a unit of linear measure mentioned frequently throughout this book, owed its very existence to accurate sky watching. This linear length of 2.722ft (82.966cm), which was used extensively to create the henges, stone circles and stone avenues for well over two millennia, was derived in great measure from planetary observation. It depended upon the length of a pendulum that was swung back and forth 366 times, whilst an observation was made of the movements of the planet Venus.

This method of establishing a linear unit was also used by the Sumerians and in both cases Venus was the target. However, both systems only worked when Venus was in a particular part of its complicated passage as seen from the Earth. It had to be an evening star and at a stage in its cycle when it appeared to be moving rapidly away from the Sun. At any other time Venus would not provide the correct information and the desired linear unit would not be accurate.

There were then many reasons why humanity, even at this early stage, would have wanted to be as accurate as possible in their understanding of planetary movement and the reason we know for sure that the Minoans were scrupulously exact in their sky watching is because the number of cycles used on the Phaistos Disc demonstrates the fact.

## Zodiac Signs and Elements

Despite the fact that astronomers are so derisive about the aims and objectives of astrology, astrology itself tends to be something of a time capsule. Unlike astronomy, its basic operating principles have not altered across many centuries and in some ways across thousands of years. The sky watchers of old were not content with simply looking at 12 totally different zodiac signs, each with its own peculiarities and attributes. They were certain that there were subtle relationships between groups of zodiac signs. This related in part to what were known as elements.

It was part of ancient thinking that everything in the world responded to one of four different elements. These were fire, earth, air and water. Some cultures had five elements, and across time they varied, but astrology tells us that whoever quantified the study thousands of years ago accepted that there were four. One of these elements was attached to each of the zodiac signs, as follows: Aries – fire, Taurus – earth, Gemini – air, Cancer – water, Leo – fire, Virgo – earth, Libra – air, Scorpio – water, Sagittarius – fire, Capricorn – earth, Aquarius – air and Pisces – water.

It was suggested, and still is by astrologers, that each of the zodiac signs, together with the people, objects and circumstances to which it related, responded to its element. People born under the influence of Aries were said to be fiery by nature – impulsive and quick – whereas those born under the influence of Taurus were earthy and stubborn, and so on. There was a time when even medicine was based on a supposed knowledge of the elements and it was a study that was taken extremely seriously for many centuries.

Because I knew about historical astronomy and astrology, I was conversant with the idea of elements and I had studied them extensively in my own research into ancient astronomy. It always seemed to me that in addition to anything they might tell our ancient ancestors about the 'nature' of people and things, they also enjoyed a deliberate mathematical purpose. It seemed as though their presence was telling me something about 'mechanism', as much as explaining any fundamental truth regarding people or objects, though for a long time I could not quantify something that was simply a gut feeling. It took my relationship with the Phaistos Disc and with the Megalithic system of geometry and measurement to bring me to a true understanding of the most important aspect of elements to ancient astronomy.

# Phaistos Disc: Number Systems

Side A of the Phaistos Disc has 123 symbols. This appeared to me to be a very significant number. We have already seen that the disc represented the mechanism for establishing a frighteningly accurate calendar, which could measure both the sidereal and tropical years, but it began to occur to me that the number sequences used on the disc could do much more.

It is almost certain that the names of the zodiac signs used by the Minoans, and doubtless also the Megalithic cultures of the far west of Europe, were the same names given to the months of the year. This would be common sense because the Sun moved at 1° per day in the 366° system and so would traverse each zodiac sign in a month. In addition, zodiac signs have always been termed as either 'positive' or 'negative' alternately. This might be a legacy of the fact that half the months were of 31 days and the other half were of 30 days. The situation may have worked as follows:

| | | | |
|---|---|---|---|
| Aries | 31 days | Sun travels 31° | positive |
| Taurus | 30 days | Sun travels 30° | negative |
| Gemini | 31 days | Sun travels 31° | positive |
| Cancer | 30 days | Sun travels 30° | negative |
| Leo | 31 days | Sun travels 31° | positive |
| Virgo | 30 days | Sun travels 30° | negative |
| Libra | 31 days | Sun travels 31° | positive |
| Scorpio | 30 days | Sun travels 30° | negative |
| Sagittarius | 31 days | Sun travels 31° | positive |
| Capricorn | 30 days | Sun travels 30° | negative |
| Aquarius | 31 days | Sun travels 31° | positive |
| Pisces | 30 days | Sun travels 30° | negative |

# The 123 Days – The Sun

I reasoned that the 123 days indicated by side A of the Disc would represent the Sun passing through four zodiac signs, which would equal 122 days, plus one extra day. This seemed significant because it meant, as an example, that if a 123-day cycle began at 1° of Aries, it would end at 2° of Leo. Aries and Leo are related signs because they both carry the element of fire. This turned out to be the working matrix of an ingenious and very simple way of establishing at what degree of which zodiac sign the Sun would be on any day, not just in one cycle of 123 days, but any. For interested readers the whole procedure is set out with examples in my book *The Bronze Age Computer Disc*.[4]

The procedure also allowed for adjusting the result to not only include the degree of a zodiac sign that the Sun would occupy on any given day, but was applicable to any hour of that day, with a result that would offer the Sun's zodiac position in degrees, minutes and even seconds of arc.

# The Moon and Planets

Although I didn't realize the fact until very recently, it is also possible to use side B of the disc to track the zodiac movements of the Moon, which, considering the speed at which the Moon moves, is a fearsome task. And perhaps even more surprising, another system exists within the number sequences of the disc that allows any interested party to ascertain the zodiac position

---

4    Alan Butler, *The Bronze Age Computer Disc*, Quantum, 1999.

of the planets Mercury and Venus on any day – ever. This too is explained in *The Bronze Age Computer Disc*.

# Eclipse Prediction

Eclipses have always been a source of both awe and fear to humanity. The fact that the body of the Sun can be completely obscured, in the midst of the day, or that the surface of the Moon can appear to turn blood red, must have brought terror to countless peoples. To us these occurrences are easily understood as an expression of the relative movements of the Earth and Moon and the way they interact, relative to the Sun, but this knowledge across humanity as a whole is very recent.

In any ancient culture, those who understood the complicated cycles upon which eclipses worked had a powerful weapon when it came to manipulating the masses. A priest or king could use an impending eclipse to frighten the populace or to prove his own power in being able to make the happening go away. The Babylonians went to great trouble to understand eclipse cycles, which are based upon an excellent understanding of the movements of the Moon. With the system of geometry and time keeping they used, this must have been a very time-consuming exercise, though for the Minoan/ Megalithic systems it was child's play.

Eclipses can be tracked by way of what is known as the Saros cycle. Although consisting of ferociously complicated Moon–Earth interactions, the relatively simple result is that if an eclipse takes place today, another, similar eclipse is most likely to take place 18 years and 11 days from today. For the Minoans and the Megalithic people, with their 366-day year, predicting them was easy. With this calendar, if an eclipse took place today, the next in the same series would follow in 18 years, less two days. Since eclipses can only take place at the time of the full Moon, the date of the occurrence would be obvious.

## One Disc of Many

Although it is impossible to prove either way, it does not appear that the Minoan disc we possess – the Phaistos Disc – was custom-designed to serve these purposes for all time spans. The symbols present on the disc seem to demonstrate that the Phaistos Disc was a 'one-off' example, set to measure astronomy across a specific 40-year period. However, since the disc is representative of a methodology, it can be applied to any period of time – just as long as the state of the sky at the starting point is known.

There could originally have been many more than one Phaistos Disc. It would have made sense to commit a particular period to a specific disc. The one that was found at Phaistos, Crete, was doubtless the example that was being used, and which was therefore operative, at a specific point in Minoan history. Sadly, it is impossible to date exactly which 40-year period this was.

## Committed to Memory

It is not out of the question that the Phaistos Disc was meant to represent a training device, used by priests to instil the systems into the minds of acolytes. This would make great sense of the fact that only one such disc was discovered. It seems perfectly reasonable to suggest that all of the systems inferred by the disc, which work perfectly and very simply, were learned and understood by those whose duty it was to study the sky and to set the calendar.

It might seem absurd to suggest that it would be possible to hold, within one human mind, the algorithms necessary to specify the zodiac position of the Sun, the Moon and the inner planets accurately, for any time of any day in the future – or indeed the past – and also be able to accurately predict eclipses. Until very recently this sort of information was stored in books of tables, known as 'ephemerides', with one slim volume being necessary for every year. Now it is achieved by way of computer algorithms. In my opinion ephemerides were necessary for two reasons.

1.  Literacy became commonplace, especially amongst the class of people that studied astrology and astronomy. It was therefore convenient to compile lists of tables itemizing Sun, Moon and planetary positions.
2.  The version of geometry and time keeping used in the modern world is a composite of two different systems. It has become so bastardized from the original Minoan/ Megalithic system that it is no longer suited to the shorthand calculations that were once so simple.

I am convinced that I have not yet fully appreciated the shorthand methods for using this system of geometry and calendar cycles, but even at my present level of understanding I am confident that a sufficiently committed priesthood could quite easily have retained all the information necessary to be excellent naked-eye astronomers who could predict Sun, Moon and planetary positions, as well as eclipse cycles from memory.

Even after so many years of reverse engineering, the more I study the number systems upon which the Phaistos Disc works, the greater are the number of accomplishments in astronomical prediction that spring from the Minoan/Megalithic calendar cycles and geometry.

# Index

Numbers in italics indicate illustrations.

# Index

Antigonus II Gonatas, King 141
Antikythera 158–9
Antikythera Mechanism
  amalgam of knowledge 201
  Ancient Greek engineering capability
    160
  astronomical device 160
  clockwork device 161, 164
  comparison of gearbox to year length
    164
  computer simulations of 160
  *The Cosmos in the Antikythera*
    *Mechanism* 165
  discovery 159–60
  evolution 162
  functions of 163
  gear trains and wheels 159, 162, 163–4
  genius of 162–3, 163–4, 164–5
  instruction manual 161
  knowledge required for creation 166
  loss of accuracy 165, 166
  needle files 161–2
  phases of the Moon 163
  prediction of eclipses 163
  sophistication 160, 162
Aratus
  accounts of the heavens 143
  background 141
  corroboration by Professor S
    Zhitomirsky 144
  length of *Phaenomena* 182
  outdated version of the sky 147
  *Phaenomena* hidden for 1500 years 155
  recreation of observations of Eudoxus
    142, 143
  relevance of number 732 145–6
'Aratus "phaenomena": Dating and
    Proving its Primary Source' 144
archaeology 20
  ancestral possessions 190–1
  astroarchaeology 101–3
  cataloguing the past 21
  collections 20–1, 22
  conservative characteristics of 191–2,
    192–3
  historical artefacts 190
  innovations and scientific
    improvements 190
  Megalithic yard and 102–3, 192–3
  ritual activity 191
  Stonehenge and 192

study of past lives 72
treasure hunters 20, 22
  *see also* Evans, Sir Arthur
architecture, classical 1–2, 6
arcs 148
Ashmolean Museum 25, 25–6
astroarchaeology 101–3
astrology 218–19, 219–20
astronomy 6, 218–19, 221
Athens
  democracy 127
  education and learning 127, 127–8
  luxuries from around the world 128
Atlantis
  conflation of different stories 136
  date of existence 131
  earthquakes and floods 131
  evolution of story 139
  fallout from Santorini volcanic
    eruption 139
  greatest civilisation 130–1
  lack of written accounts 139
  myth of 132–3, 139
  size and location 131
  waging war 131

Babylonians
  eclipse cycles and predictions 166,
    224
  fractions 166, 167
Basques
  geography of region 78–9
  language 76–7, 198–9
blacksmithing 162
boats
  'cobbles' 57
  early made 55, 56
  Ferriby 56, 57
  Minoan-built 57
British Isles
  agriculture in 119–20
  Celtic tribes *see* Celts
  communal projects 18–19, 118–19
  conflict and tribal divisions 120
  geography and climate 15
  henges 17–18, 109, 119, 185
  influx of 'Beaker people.' 79
  pottery and tools 79
  Roman period 15–16
  Stone and Bronze Ages 16–17
  stone circles 18

# Index

# Index